Rea~
Steady!
Assembly!

Claire Derry & Helen Franklin

Scripture Union

First published 1998

Scripture Union, 207–209 Queensway, Bletchley, Milton Keynes, MK2 2EB, England.

ISBN 1 85999 189 0

British Library Cataloguing-in-Publication Data.
A catalogue record of this book is available from the British Library.

Printed and bound in Great Britain by
Ebenezer Baylis & Son Ltd, Worcester and London.

CONTENTS

LIST OF CONTRIBUTORS AND ACKNOWLEDGEMENTS

Esther Bailey (22, 28, 32, 33, 34, 35, 36)
Claire Derry (1, 2, 3, 4, 10, 11, 13, 14, 16, 18, 19, 20, 23)
Colin Draper (21, 30)
Helen Franklin (6, 8, 9, 15, 24, 26, 27, 30, 31, 38, 39, 40, 41)
Bruce Lockhart (17)
John Marshall (25, 29)
Julie Sharp (5, 7, 12)
Cathie Smith (37)

The Egyptian rap for assembly 14 is from an issue of *Learning Together*, Scripture Union

The story of Nicodemus in assembly 18 came from *The Lion Children's Bible*, retold by Pat Alexander, text © 1981,1991 Lion Publishing plc.

The original Luke Street stories that provide the basis for Section 5, were written by David Lewis from narratives in the gospels.

The original ideas for the assembly 34 came from *Thank you for a loaf of bread*, Patricia & Victor Smeltzer, Lion Publishing (out of print).

The artwork for assembly 2 is by Katie Wormald.
The artwork for assembly 16 is taken from the original *Shipmates* holiday club material, SU Missions Department.

Some of the introductory material came from *Everyone Matters* by Tricia Williams, published by Scripture Union.

SOURCE BOOKS FOR RECOMMENDED SONGS:

Big Blue Planet, Stainer & Bell and Methodist Church Division of Education and Youth, 1995
Everybody Praise, ICC/Scripture Union, 1997
Junior Praise, Marshall Pickering, 1992
Someone's Singing, Lord, A&C Black Ltd, 1973
Spring Harvest Kids Praise 88/89, ICC, 1989
Spring Harvest Kids Praise 92, ICC, 1992
Spring Harvest Kids Praise 94, ICC, 1994
Spring Harvest Kids Praise 97, ICC, 1992

Spring Harvest Kids Praise songs for 1988 to 1995 are also in a book called *The Big Book of Spring Harvest Kids Praise*, ICC, 1995 which is now out of print.

Some of the songs recommended are in more than one song book. We have given one reference only, but it is worth looking them up in your own books.

INTRODUCTION

Time and space for God

For many children assembly is the only time and space they have to think about God and his relevance to them. The statutory requirement in England and Wales[*] – that all maintained schools have daily acts of worship, the majority of which are 'wholly or mainly of a broadly Christian character' – provides an opportunity to help children begin to see beyond the values of a material world and to develop an awareness of God, who is there, who cares about them and who has given guidelines to help us live together.

This book is intended as a resource for all those who want, and are able, to take up that opportunity by leading assemblies for the 4–7 age group in primary schools – as a teacher or a visitor to school. All the outlines in this book are specifically Christian in nature.

If you're a teacher…

For many teachers the responsibility of leading assembly in an already overcrowded day is one thing they could do without, whatever their own personal faith and beliefs. In the context of school, the thirty or so children in your class and their education are your top priority. Assembly feels as if it comes much further down the list. Whatever your ideals, it may help to spend some time deliberately

[*]In Scotland the requirement for primary schools is that religious observance, which is broadly Christian in character, takes place at least once a week. In Northern Ireland the requirement for grant-aided schools is a daily act of collective worship.

considering the significance of the fact that for many children, school assembly is one of the few places where they hear about God.

Although the assemblies in this book need some preparation, it is hoped that these outlines will help you prepare and lead lively, enjoyable assemblies which will contribute to the spiritual growth and awareness of the children in your care.

If you're a visitor...

Remember you are a visitor to the school – a guest. Maybe you were responsible for making contact, but it is the school who has taken up your offer and invited you. Be a wise and courteous guest. That way you might be invited back!

- If you don't already know, find out some background information about the school and what usually happens in assembly:
  - What are the social and ethnic backgrounds of the children?
  - What other faiths, apart from Christian, are represented in the school?
  - Are assemblies in the school usually Christian in character?
  - What are staff and children used to in assembly (prayer, Bible reading, singing)?
- Check the amount of time you have for the assembly. Keep to those time limits. Order is very important in a school, where staff have the job of caring for a large number of children. Teachers also have a full day and will want to keep to their planned schedules.
- Be punctual. Allow plenty of time if you need to set up equipment or props in the hall before the assembly begins.
- Be flexible. Schools don't always run like clockwork. If someone has forgotten that you were coming, or that half the children would be on a school trip, or that the OHP was stolen in the break-in last week – don't panic, but do be prepared.
- Prepare your assembly well. The school is placing their trust in you in allowing you to lead an assembly.
- Dress in a way which won't draw unhelpful attention to yourself. You want the children (and staff) to be talking at break-time about the content of the assembly, not about the clothes you were wearing (unless they were a deliberate part of the assembly)!
- During the assembly, don't over-excite the children. If they do get excited, make sure you include a calming down slot as well. Remember that teachers have to help them settle to classroom work afterwards.

• If you make any kind of mess in the assembly (paper on the floor, food spilt etc), offer to clear up afterwards.

• Remember that this is a school assembly – not a family service at church or Sunday school. Remember the diverse backgrounds of the children; the fact that most of them will have no involvement with a church; and the responsibility of the school towards the children – to educate, not indoctrinate.

• Remember that your presentation of Christian truth is part of a wider picture. There are others who regularly lead assemblies and there will be children from Christian families who unconsciously communicate Christian values. Religious Education is part of the curriculum and there may be a Christian group functioning in the school. All these different aspects are bringing the reality of God into the life of the school community.

• Ideally, it will be possible for you to take more than one assembly. With regular involvement you can begin to build up a relationship with the children and the staff of the school.

The children

• The children facing you in an assembly come from a wide variety of family situations and social, ethnic and religious backgrounds. Be aware of this as you prepare your material.

• Don't assume knowledge of the Christian faith. Don't put words of belief or commitment into the mouths of children who will want to please you but who don't fully understand the meaning of those words. Be respectful of the feelings of the parents of children who hold different faiths, even though you may not agree with their beliefs.

• Most four to seven year olds inhabit a world of literal concepts. Avoid abstract ideas and concepts.

• Children of this age are inquisitive and open. They are eager to discover and understand more of their world.

• Four to seven year olds are very trusting of adults – especially any who appear to be in a position of responsibility, like taking an assembly. Make sure what you tell them is trustworthy and true.

• Children of this age enjoy talking and hearing about their immediate world: their families, school, friends in their street, children's TV, the latest toys, games, books, films, music etc. Use illustrations from their world.

- Children love to laugh. Use humour in your illustrations but never make fun of a child in the assembly.

Distinctive qualities of infant assemblies

If you have ever taught in or visited an Infant School for an assembly, or been part of an 'Infants only' assembly in a Primary School, you will be aware that they are very different from a junior assembly where Infants and Juniors are present together.
But what makes them different? I would suggest that it is the characteristics of the 4–7 age group.

Children of this age think very much in the here and now. They need things phrased in everyday language. They are very spontaneous and enthusiastic. They are creative and responsive. Their world still revolves very much around themselves, although some are beginning to think of others.

Those leading infant assemblies are able to focus on relating to the world of a 4–7 year old without talking over the top of their heads in language too hard for them to understand. They can use the appropriate vocabulary and manner in addressing young children, which will encourage maximum participation by the children.

Infant children are in general more responsive in the assembly situation, if the assembly is geared at their level. Some reception children have not yet learnt not to call out and this whole age group enjoys the more interactive-type assembly where they can join in and be very much a part of the whole proceedings. Children of this age have a very short concentration span and an interactive assembly helps them to concentrate for longer!

Those leading assemblies for Infants must be aware that anything can happen at any time! It could be a child desperate to tell everyone something, a child in tears, that little accident on the floor, a child falling asleep – the Infant assembly can certainly be interesting and has particular qualities of its own.

The place of collective worship in the day-to-day running of the school – How it is valued and viewed.

"The book will be outside my door if I'm busy," said the Head Teacher to the Deputy.

How high a priority is given to collective worship these days in school and how is it viewed?

So much obviously depends on a whole number of factors – the tradition of the school; the Head teacher and individual teachers; whether it is a church or county school; whether it is a multi-faith situation or not etc.

Sometimes collective worship is held simply because schools have an obligation to fulfil the law. Sometimes collective worship is solely a 'coming together' with no religious content at all, at any time. Sometimes the collective worship in a school will be led only by the Head teacher or Deputy who often read from a book of assemblies which they work their way through.

However in many schools great care and effort is taken over what happens in collective worship. Teachers attend courses, have inset days on this subject, are allowed money for resources. Thoughtful planning ahead means themes are worked out for each term or half term, visitors and class assemblies are slotted in, making the short time each day a rich experience, a time which often reflects the whole 'ethos' or atmosphere of the school.

USING THIS BOOK

Aim:

Every assembly should have one clear point, and this is stated at the start of each outline as the aim. Keep this in mind as you lead the assembly and be sure to communicate it clearly.

Bible base:

Each outline has a Bible base, the passage which is behind the story or teaching point. Read this as part of your preparation, but you do not need to read it out as part of the assembly unless the outline tells you to do so.

You will need:

Check this list far enough in advance to allow yourself time to assemble any props or equipment needed. If you intend to use an overhead projector, check first that the school has one. If using electrical equipment of your own it is always helpful to take an extension lead too in case there is no socket nearby.

Preparation

Practical preparation is explained in each outline, but the most important preparation is to be familiar with the material:

*   fix the aim in your head;
*   rehearse any stories and prepare visuals;
*   decide where any prayers and songs will come (they are listed at the end of each outline, but this may not always be the best place); check that you have the music if someone else is to play songs for you;

- anticipate what answers the children may give to any questions you ask, and consider how you might move on from them.

Presentation

1   Think through in advance what your very first words will be – how you will greet the children or whether you need to leap straight into the story, eg if you are playing the part of a particular character. Many of the assemblies have an introduction that creates interest and links today's world with the Bible story to be told. But beware of spending so long on the introduction that there is no time for the story!

2   Visuals have been suggested in some outlines because they help children to remember better the aim of the assembly. Don't despair if you can't draw; either find someone who can produce a simple line drawing for you or use a book such as *How To Cheat At Visual Aids*, published by Scripture Union. Take into account the size of room in which you will be working and make sure that pictures can be seen from a distance.

3   Practise telling any story out loud so that you are confident with how it will sound; if you want to memorise it, concentrate most on the beginning and the end. That way you will usually remember the middle too. See Lance Pierson's book *Storytelling*, published by Scripture Union, for more help.

4   If you choose children to take part, give clear directions and tell them when their part is over and they can sit down. If you do not know the children well it may be better to ask a member of staff to select volunteers for you. Be prepared that anything might happen! If all the children are to join in certain words, rehearse them before you tell the story. Remember that infants *may* get carried away when helping to make noises! Work out in advance how you will quieten them down, eg a hand signal, and tell them what this is.

5   If a child answers a question for you, thank them for their answer and repeat it briefly so that everyone has heard it. Work out how to handle any wrong answers so that you boost the confidence of the child and value their contribution, but are able to move on to the correct answer.

Prayer

Prayer allows children the opportunity to reflect on what they have heard and seen, and to respond to it. It need not be spoken out loud, but if you ask children to think quietly, give them some idea of what they might think about, and keep the time relatively short. Encourage children to join in at the end with 'Amen' if they agree with what you have said in a spoken prayer. Be sensitive to the fact that there may be children present with different religious backgrounds, or whose families have no religious belief. Don't make children say something that they don't mean.

Song suggestions

Where possible, use a song that fits with the theme of the assembly. Be ready to give way on this if the school have been practising one especially to sing that day! As before, don't make children sing words that they don't mean. Try to avoid songs that say "I believe.."; choose those that are factual, eg "God is...".

And finally...

As you prepare, think carefully of the words that you will use to end the assembly or to hand back to the teacher in charge. I have ruined some by a throwaway remark as I have gone to sit down! End on a positive, happy note.

SECTION 1

SPECIAL PEOPLE

1 RED SEA RESCUE

Aim: To show the children that God has power over his creation.

Bible base: Exodus 14

You will need:

- Simple picture clues drawn either on acetates or on large sheets of paper
- A stick to represent the one Moses had (You could use a walking stick.)
- Two large flash cards: 'Egyptians' and 'Israelites'
- A cassette player and a tape of God's words to Moses

Preparation

- Prepare simple picture clues on acetates or paper, similar to the game 'Dingbats'. Examples: Bluebell (draw a bell and colour it blue), Happy Birthday (draw a smiley face followed by a birthday cake), Baa baa black sheep (draw Babar the elephant followed by a sheep coloured in black), Red Sea (draw the letter 'C' and colour it red).
- Prepare the two flash cards, 'Egyptians' and 'Israelites'.
- Record on a cassette tape God's words to Moses in Exodus 14:16. 'Moses, lift up your stick and hold it out over the sea. The water will divide, and the Israelites will be able to walk through the sea on dry ground.'
- If possible, before the assembly begins conceal the tape recorder and have a teacher lined up to operate this on cue.

Presentation

Introduction

1   Have fun playing the picture clue game, where the children must say what they see. Do one or two for them until they grasp how to play. End with the red 'C'.

2   Use this last clue to lead into the story. Ask the children if they know where the Red Sea is.

Story

1 Begin with the background:

The Israelites, God's special people, had been slaves in Egypt. The Pharaoh, who was like the king, had decided to let them go free, so they had set out into the desert and reached the Red Sea. The Pharaoh changed his mind and chased them with his great army. The Israelites were trapped. They turned to Moses their leader in panic.

2 Choose a group of children to be Israelites and a group to be Egyptians, one child from each group holding up the appropriate flash card. Choose a child to be Moses.

3 Tell the story from Exodus 14 very simply, using the children to act it out as you go and using the tape recording at the appropriate point.

Application

1 Ask the children how Moses and the Israelites must have felt when they realised they were trapped.

2 Point out to the children that they prayed to God for help and he rescued them. What did he do?

Time to reflect

1 Ask the children to be very still and close their eyes for a few moments and to think how powerful God must be to have done this.

2 Remind them that God made the world and everything in it. He can tell seas what to do!

Song suggestion

• How did Moses cross the Red Sea? 83, *Junior Praise*

2 WHO? ME?

Aim: To show the children that God can use anyone to do his work.

Bible base: Judges 6

You will need:

- The following props for the introduction – comb and mirror, glasses and maths text book, 2 litre orange squash bottle filled with water
- Four photocopiable acetates or large pieces of paper
- An OHP if using acetates

Preparation

- Photocopy pictures 1–4 (pages 6–9) onto acetates or enlarge on paper.
- Familiarise yourself beforehand with the story of God calling Gideon. (The main points are outlined below and the pictures will help you as you go along.)

Presentation

Introduction
1 Ask for three volunteers.
2 Give them the following or similar names: Beautiful Brenda (give her the comb and mirror); Clever Chloe (give her the glasses and book); Super-strong Sam (give him the heavy container of water).
3 Introduce each character in turn, encouraging your volunteers to mime a little using their props.

Story
Lead into the story by saying that today they will hear about a time when God chose someone to do a very important job for him, but he wasn't particularly good-looking, clever or strong!

PICTURE I
God's people, the Israelites, had forgotten about God and done wrong things. Some enemies had kept coming to steal their animals and food. The Israelites had run away and hidden in some caves in the hills.

PICTURE 2
One day a young man called Gideon was secretly threshing some wheat when suddenly an angel appeared and spoke to him.

'God is with you brave and mighty man,' said the angel. Gideon was very surprised. 'God has chosen you to free your people from their enemies.' 'Who? Me?' said Gideon, 'But I'm the youngest in my family, and we're not a very important family.' Gideon couldn't believe it, but the angel told him that God had promised to be with him and help him. The angel disappeared and Gideon was left to think about all that had been said.

PICTURE 3
Gideon took a trumpet and blew it. Soon a whole army had gathered to help Gideon fight their enemies.

Then Gideon wondered whether God really would be with him and help him. He asked God to prove it. Gideon put out some wool on the ground. He said to God, 'If in the morning the dew is only on the wool and not on the ground around it, I will know that you have chosen me and will be with me.' The next day it was just as Gideon had asked; the wool was wet with dew and the ground dry.

PICTURE 4
But Gideon was still not sure, so he spoke to God again. 'Please don't be cross, let me make one more test with the wool. This time let the wool be dry and the ground be wet.' God did that very thing. The wool was dry but the ground was wet.

Application
Ask the children:

Why didn't Gideon think he could fight the enemies?
What did God think of Gideon?
What had God promised Gideon?

Prayer

Invite the children to listen to the following prayer, and if they agree and want to make it their prayer too, to say 'Amen' at the end. You could use these or similar words:

Outline continued on page 26

Dear God, thank you that we are all important to you.
Thank you that you have promised to be with us and help us.

Song suggestion

- There is no-one else like you, 476, *Junior Praise*

3 FOR GOD AND FOR GIDEON!

Aim: To show the children that God is so great, he can do anything.

Bible base: Judges 7

You will need:

- A Superman logo
- A large sheet of paper
- Three flash cards
- An earthenware jar or jug
- A torch
- A trumpet (real, toy or cardboard cut-out)

Preparation

- Draw an outline of the Superman logo in the centre of the large sheet of paper (if possible display on a flip chart or board).
- Prepare flash cards with the numbers 32,000, 10,000 and 300.

Presentation

Introduction

Show the children the Superman logo and ask them if they recognise it. Discuss with them the special things that super-heroes can do, eg fly, x-ray vision, etc. Write these up as you go along.

Story

Gideon was no super-hero, but he was the man God had chosen to free his people from their enemies and God had promised to be with him.

Gideon had gathered a huge army of 32,000 men (*ask a child out to hold up the flash card*) but God told him the army was too big. God said that they might think they had won by themselves without his help if they had all those men!

God told Gideon to tell anyone who was frightened to go home. 22,000 men went home leaving Gideon with only 10,000 (*next flash card held up*). But God still said that there were too many, so he told Gideon what to do. All the men had to go down to the river and have a drink. All those who got down and cupped the water in their hands were to stay but those who knelt down and put their face in the water to drink were to be sent home. This left Gideon with only 300 men (*next flash card held up*)!

So Gideon divided the 300 men into groups of 100, each man carrying a torch, a jar and a trumpet (*show the props explaining the differences between these and the ones Gideon's army would have used*). At midnight they surrounded the enemy camp.

When Gideon gave the signal they all blew their trumpets, smashed their jars and waved their torches shouting, 'For God and for Gideon!' Their enemies were so afraid they all ran away yelling!

Time to reflect

1 Ask the children to be still and close their eyes.

2 Remind them again that Gideon was just someone very ordinary who trusted God.

3 Also emphasise God's greatness, his amazing power in helping Gideon and his men to win.

Prayer

Invite the children to say 'Amen' at the end if they wish to.

Dear God, thank you that you are mighty and powerful.
Thank you that you can do absolutely anything. Amen.

Song suggestion

• God's people aren't super-brave super-heroes, 5, *Spring Harvest Kids' Praise 1997*

4   STICKING TOGETHER

Aim: To show that God is pleased when we are good friends.

Bible base: Ruth

You will need:

- A selection of methods of sticking things together, eg *Blu-tack*, staples, sticky tape, superglue
- Some small pieces of paper, card, material, wool to stick together
- Two sticks and strips of card
- 5 paper plates for 'plate head' puppets

Preparation

- Make two signposts (strips of card stuck to a stick), one saying 'Bethlehem', the other 'Moab'.
- Make 'plate head' puppets to represent Naomi, Orpah, Ruth, Boaz and Obed. Draw faces on paper plates with marker pens and add material, wool for hair, beards etc.
- Read through the story outline below to familiarise yourself with it.

Presentation

Introduction

1   Talk to the children about different ways of sticking things together. Demonstrate a few using the methods you have brought. Allow the children time to make suggestions themselves.

2   Finish with the superglue method emphasising how difficult it is to separate the pieces of card stuck together with this. Tell the children that some people are such good friends that they 'stick together' whatever happens. Today they will hear about a woman in the Bible who stuck with her friend even when things were difficult.

Story

1   You could invite children out to hold up the different puppets and signposts as you tell the story.

2   Introduce the children to your Naomi puppet and show them your 'Bethlehem' signpost. Tell the story:

> Naomi lived in the town of Bethlehem with her husband Elimelech and her two sons. Things were looking bad for the family, as the fields in Bethlehem were dry and dusty, there was no food left to eat and everyone was hungry. Elimelech decided it was time to leave and move to a place where there was food.
>
> So all the family went on a very long journey to the country of Moab and settled there.

3   (*Show 'Moab' signpost.*)

> The two sons grew up and married two girls from Moab, called Ruth and Orpah.

4   (*Introduce your Ruth and Orpah puppets.*)

> Sadly, Elimelech died and then about ten years later Naomi's two sons died, leaving her all alone. Naomi had heard that there was now food in Bethlehem, so she decided she would go back home.

5   (*Hold up 'Bethlehem' signpost.*)

> Ruth and Orpah couldn't leave Naomi to make the long journey on her own so they decided to go with her. As they travelled along, Naomi tried very hard to tell Ruth and Orpah to go back and eventually Orpah kissed Naomi goodbye and went back to Moab.

6   (*Hold up 'Moab' signpost.*)

> But Ruth just wouldn't leave Naomi so they travelled on together.
>
> When they reached Bethlehem it was harvest time and the farmers were beginning to bring in the crops. Naomi's old friends were so pleased to see her, but Naomi was sad – her husband and sons were dead.
>
> Naomi and Ruth were very poor. Ruth would go out into the fields each day and pick up any leftover pieces of corn. Ruth didn't know that she was working in a field which belonged to a rich relative of Naomi's. His name was Boaz.

7   (*Show your Boaz puppet.*)

Boaz found out that Ruth was a foreigner and was very kind to her. Boaz married Ruth and they had a beautiful baby son called Obed.

8   (*Hold up Obed puppet and then Bethlehem sign.*)
Ruth who had been such a good friend to Naomi was the happiest woman in Bethlehem!

Application
1   Ask the children why they think Ruth stuck with Naomi.
2   Talk about how hard it must have been for her in a strange land, far away from the people she knew.
3   Make the point that being a good friend isn't always easy – sometimes it will be difficult to keep on being friends. God is happy when we are good friends.

Prayer

Thank you, God, for friends. Help us to be good friends who stick with each other whatever happens. Amen.

Song suggestion

• Isn't it good?, 45, *Everybody Praise*

5 CARMEL COMPETITION

Aim:

To help the children understand that God is the only God, the greatest, and he's real!

Bible base:

1 Kings 18:1–40

You will need:

- Some items which the children are likely to choose between, for example, an apple and an orange, a football and a book, some *Smarties* and a tube of fruit pastilles
- A few simple props for the story, for example, a crown for Ahab, a cloak for Elijah, a bucket etc

Preparation

- Familiarise yourself with the story from 1 Kings: 18 and look carefully at the script so as to know how to use your volunteers.

Presentation

Introduction

1   Discuss with the children times they have made decisions. Are there times when it's difficult to make up your mind?
2   Show the children your items which they may have had to choose between.

Background

1   Explain to the children that God's people the Israelites had many bad kings. Probably the worst king was King Ahab, and his wife Jezebel was even nastier than him!
2   Ahab did not care about God. Jezebel worshipped a false god called Baal and soon the people were so confused that they could not make up their minds about God at all.
3   God had already sent one message by his special messenger Elijah to try and make Ahab listen. There had been no rain for three years, Ahab was in a foul mood and God sent Elijah to Ahab again.

Story

Choose some volunteers to help you tell the story:

a King Ahab, an Elijah, a few prophets of Baal, all the other children in the assembly will be the crowd watching the competition which takes place.

Story script:

When Ahab and Elijah met, Ahab was so angry he could hardly keep still.

(*Have Ahab and Elijah standing facing one another, Ahab shaking with rage!*)

He was twitching and shaking with anger

'You have caused this trouble!' Ahab shrieked, his voice shrill and squeaking.

'No, it's not me,' said Elijah. 'You have forgotten to take any notice of God. Now he is going to show you something more about himself.

Get all the people to Mount Carmel.

Get all the prophets of Baal together.

Collect everyone in one big crowd.

There's going to be a competition.'

Soon a huge crowd of people were gathered and 450 prophets of Baal, all ready for a big competition.

(*Elijah faces the rest of the children.*)

'Listen,' said Elijah to the people. 'You've got to make up your minds who you think is real. You can't be on God's side and Baal's side. You've got to choose.'

But the people said nothing.

They had heard there was a competition coming and they wanted to see it.

'OK,' said Elijah, 'bring out two bulls.' The people obeyed. Normally bulls were burned as a sacrifice to God to show respect and honour, like a kind of present.

(*Ask a volunteer to mime bringing out the sacrifice.*)

'The competition will be to see which god brings down fire to burn the sacrifice,' said Elijah. 'Do you agree?'

The prophets of Baal stamped and shouted and whooped and made a great noise.

(*Prophets of Baal stamp, shout, whoop, etc.*)

'It that a yes?' said Elijah.

'Yes!' they roared.

(*Prophets and Elijah mime appropriately as the story continues.*)

The prophets put the large piece of meat on a pile of stones and started to pray.

'Baal hear us! Baal hear us! Bring fire – and make it hot!' (*Prophets could say this after you.*) But nothing happened.

So they yelled, 'Baal hear us! Baal hear us! Bring fire and make it snappy!'

But nothing happened. 'Perhaps he's out with a friend? Or shopping? Or on the loo?' suggested Elijah, smiling.

The prophets of Baal went crazy: dancing and leaping and screaming. But nothing happened.

Hours passed.

Elijah said very quietly to the people, 'Gather round.' And they did. He built a pile of twelve stones, put on the wood and put the meat on top. Then he asked for a spade. He dug a deep ditch round the stones and asked for a bucket of water.

'Water?' said the people. 'He's definitely crazy.'

Elijah poured water over the meat. Splash!

'Doesn't he realise?' said a little old woman. 'It'll never cook like that.'

Elijah poured on water a second time. Splash.

And a third time. Swoosh.

Water trickled down into the deep ditch. 'When God wins this competition,' said Elijah, 'it will NOT be by chance.'

'Now God,' he said, 'show these people that you *are* alive, that you are the greatest, that you are the only God, that you are the REAL THING.'

Then God sent fire – it licked up the water like a hungry beast. Flames roared round the stones, the wood, the meat and leapt red and yellow into the sky. When all the people saw this they jumped up in surprise.

'Wow!' they yelled. 'It's amazing.'

Then they knelt down.

'It's true. God is the only God, the real thing. God is the greatest.'

Time to reflect

1   Ask the children to think about the story they have just heard and seen.

2   Ask them to think about what they will decide or have decided about God.

Prayer

Invite the children to join in the following prayer (or similar) by saying 'Amen' if they wish to:

> *Dear God, help us to know that you are real and with us even though we can't see you with our eyes, hear you with our ears or touch you with our hands. Thank you that you are the one true God, the greatest, the real thing. Amen.*

Song Suggestion

* My Lord is higher than a mountain, 170, *Junior Praise*

6 THE FIERY FURNACE

Aim:

To show the children that God is more powerful than anyone or anything.

Bible base:

Daniel 3

You will need:

- Pictures of powerful people eg prime minister, president, queen/king, etc
- Some flame-coloured clothing to wear – reds, oranges, yellows and/or a cardboard headband with brightly coloured flame shapes attached to it to make a hat

Preparation

- Familiarise yourself with script of story, if possible learn it.
- Dress in the coloured clothing.

Presentation

Introduction

- Ask the children who they think is the most powerful person in the world.
- Let the children look at the different pictures you have brought in and talk about how there was a king in the Bible who thought that he was more powerful than anyone else in the world, but discovered he wasn't.
- Tell the children that you will pretend to be something in the story and tell them all about it (*put on your hat!*).

Story

Use the following script to tell the story:

> Hello! I don't suppose you've ever met a talking fiery furnace before. I'm a bit special, because something amazing once happened in me. Let me tell you all about it.

I work in Babylon, a country far away from here, whose king was called Nebuchadnezzar. What a name, eh?! I don't suppose anyone here is called Nebuchadnezzar!

Well, I have a very important job to do. I burn all the rubbish that people no longer want – old vegetable peelings, clothes that are too scruffy and torn even for cleaning rags, never mind for people to wear again, bits of broken things from people's homes – you know the sort of stuff, anything that can never be used again and is now just rubbish.

One day, as my door was open whilst people were putting in rubbish for me to burn up, I heard three men talking.

'Have you seen that statue that the king has had put up? Nearly twenty-seven metres high and three metres wide! And it's all gold! Imagine that!' said one of the men.

'Yes, Shadrach, and do you know what the king has demanded?' asked another. 'That whenever we hear the special music play we must all bow down and worship it.'

'Worship it?' cried the third man. 'Never! We should worship only God.'

'OK, Abednego,' said the second man. 'What do you suggest we do?'

'Well, Meshach, we must refuse to bow down to the statue, and if the king doesn't like it, tough! If we are punished for it, God will save us. And even if he doesn't, we are still not going to bow down to the king's statue.'

And off they went, Shadrach, Meshach and Abednego.

Some days later, I heard a lot of noise nearby and my doors were pulled wide open. I recognised the voice that was shouting the loudest: it was King Nebuchadnezzar!

'Put more coals on the fire!' he commanded. And the men did.

'More!' shouted the king. 'Much more!' I grew hotter and hotter until I was seven times hotter than usual.

Well, by now I was so hot that I was dangerous. You know how careful you have to be with fire. The doors opened again and I expected the rubbish to be thrown in. But imagine my horror when not rubbish, but the three men, Shadrach, Meshach and Abednego, were thrown into me instead! They were all tied up and they couldn't possibly escape. If I could have cooled down quickly I would have done, but I was so hot that the soldiers who pushed the men inside were killed by my heat. And there was nothing that I could do to help them.

And then something amazing happened. Shadrach, Meshach and Abednego were not hurt by my incredible heat. They started to walk around, completely unhurt. And, even more amazing, there was a fourth man walking there with them. Who could it be? Was this their great God who I had heard them talking about?

The king came close to me and shouted, 'Shadrach, Meshach and Abednego, servants of the most high God, come out!' And they did, with not a hair on their heads touched by my fire. It was incredible! The king called to everyone to listen to him. 'Praise be to the God of Shadrach, Meshach and Abednego. These men trusted him and he has saved them.'

And that was the end of that. I'm back to burning up people's rubbish now, and everything is alright again. I thought I was powerful when they heated me up so hot. But I'll never be anything like as powerful as God.

(*Take your hat off!*)

Application

1   Comment that King Nebuchadnezzar realised that God was far more powerful than himself. Ask the children why. What did God do to show his power in the story?

2   Tell the children that Christians believe God is still as powerful as that today.

Prayer

Invite the children to say 'Amen' to this prayer if they would like to:

Father God, thank you that you have the power to do things that no ordinary person can do. Amen.

Song suggestion

*   My God is so big, so strong and so mighty, 169, *Junior Praise*

7   DANGER IN THE DEN

Aim: To help the children understand that God is always with them in whatever situation they may find themselves.

Bible base: Daniel 6

You will need:

*   Some photos of personal friends (as large as possible)
*   A few simple props to help your acting volunteers, for example a crown for King Darius, a card headband with Percy written on it, a rug, etc

Preparation

*   Look carefully at the story in Daniel 6 and at the script, noting the places props will be used.

Presentation

Introduction

1   Show the children your photos. (Those nearer the back could have a closer look later if they are unable to see.) Tell them why you enjoy being with your friends, how they may have helped you when in difficulty and about things you have done together.

2   Point out to the children that however special your friends are, they can't be with you all the time and they can't always help you.

3   Explain that Daniel, a man we read about in the Bible, found out there was only one special best friend who could always be there and always help.

Story

Choose a few volunteers to act out the story as you tell it using the props where appropriate.

> A long time ago in a distant land,
> many hundreds and thousands of years ago,
> there was a man called Daniel,
> and a great king called Darius.

Daniel had worked for the king all his life but unlike many other men at the palace he always spoke the truth.

Also Daniel knew that God was wise, strong, loving, the greatest.
Every day, morning, midday and evening he would talk to God like a friend,
tell him about his day,
about problems at the palace,
what sort of mood the king was in,
anything and everything
and God listened.

King Darius admired Daniel and listened to everything he said carefully.
Daniel always spoke the truth
and because God had given him good advice,
he was always having brilliant new ideas.
The king always took notice of what Daniel said
and the other important people in the palace became more and more annoyed.
'Who does he think he is?'
'He makes us look stupid!'
'I hate him.'
And they began huddling together in corners of the palace grounds, trying to come up with some idea about how to get rid of Daniel.
Eventually one man, Percy, came up with a cunning plan. Although King Darius appreciated Daniel's honest approach, he was very vain and he liked people saying nice things about him.
One morning, when Daniel was out seeing to some important business for the king, Percy went into the royal apartments, threw himself down on the Persian rug and said,
'O Great and Wonderful.
I can hardly bring myself to breathe in the presence of your majesty. Please allow me to grovel at your feet.'
'Certainly, dear boy,' said the king.
'Your majesty,' Percy continued, 'the people know you are handsome, strong and very wise.'
The king smiled. 'Do they?' he said.
'But perhaps they do not know quite HOW WONDERFUL you are.'
The king frowned. 'Don't they?' he said.

'Why don't we make a new law which says the people can only pray to you and to no one else for the next thirty days?'

'Excellent, excellent,' said the king. 'Let's do it.'

Percy grinned sneakily, bowed and left the throne room.

And so it turned out that by the time Daniel came back to the palace, a new law had been written and sealed by the king and was to be enforced by a whole division of palace guards. Daniel heard about this new law as he reached the palace gates.

The king welcomed him as usual.

He told Daniel of the new law he'd devised by himself without Daniel's help.

'Congratulations, my lord king,' said Daniel. 'Tell me about it.'

So the king told him about the law and the people having to pray to him alone.

'Aah,' said Daniel, 'and what will happen to those who disobey?'

The king told him that Percy had come up with a good idea.

'Oh,' said Daniel.

'The new law says that anyone praying to someone other than me will be thrown into a pit of lions.'

'Oh dear, oh dear,' said Daniel softly.

And he kept saying this to himself as he went home, talked to God and climbed into bed.

In fact he kept on saying this to himself even in his sleep – a sleep troubled by dreams of bright eyes, golden manes and very large teeth.

The next morning, everyone started praying to the king, but Daniel talked to God instead.

At mid day, everyone still prayed to the king, but Daniel talked to God instead.

In the evening when everyone else was praying to King Darius, Daniel was talking to God.

All the people were too afraid to disobey the king.

But Daniel could not desert God, his oldest friend.

Of course, this is what Daniel's enemies wanted.

Percy and a few friends had sneaked round to Daniel's house to spy on him.

Daniel made no secret of what he was doing.

He sat by the open window, talking to God, as usual, like a friend.

After they saw this, his enemies went and told the king that Daniel was still praying three times a day. The king looked very serious and sad when they told him what had happened, but had to agree that

Daniel had broken the new law. Daniel was arrested and bundled off to the king.

Daniel said, 'I'm sorry for disobeying you, my lord king, but God is too good a friend to give up.'

The king understood, but Percy reminded him the law had been broken, a law written and signed by the king himself.

The king said to Daniel, 'May your God rescue you!' and Daniel was put into the pit where the lions lived.

The entrance was sealed and the king went back miserably to the palace.

All night King Darius walked up and down in his dressing gown.

In the morning the king was at the entrance to the pit at first light. 'Daniel, Daniel,' he called ' Was your God able to save you?'

'Yes, your majesty,' said Daniel, 'God sent an angel to shut the lions' mouths. They did not harm me at all. Isn't it wonderful? I knew God wouldn't let me down.'

The king was overjoyed to hear his friend alive and gave orders for Daniel to be pulled out of the pit. The lions roared ferociously but everyone could see that Daniel had not been hurt at all.

The king said, 'My dear Daniel, it is wonderful. This just goes to show that GOD IS THE BEST FRIEND TO HAVE after all.'

Application

1   Talk about Daniel's feelings when the law was made, when he was in the lion's den, and when the lions didn't hurt him.

2   Make the point that God is with us, as he was with Daniel. We can trust him to help us if we ask him.

Song suggestion

- Daniel was a man of prayer, 36, *Junior Praise*
- There once was a man called Daniel, 477, *Junior Praise*

SECTION 2

I'M SPECIAL

8   I MATTER

Aim: To show the children that each one of us matters as individuals.

Bible base: The Gospels

You will need:

- A selection of hats or costumes for different jobs, eg a white coat (doctor), police helmet, tweed hat (farmer), book (teacher), clock (for someone who does not have a job but has time to fill), teddy bear (child), dustbin liner (refuse collector), duster (cleaner or someone who does housework)
- You may want to have some pictures for the story at the end

Preparation

Familiarise yourself with stories from the gospels which show that all sorts of people mattered to Jesus. (See example in Story.)

Presentation

Introduction

1   Ask the children who they think is the most important person in the room. (They will probably name the head teacher.)
2   Invite some children up to the front to wear or hold the costumes and props.
3   Talk to the children about the different jobs these people do.
4   Ask who they think is the most important, and why.
5   We sometimes think that some people are more important than others because of the jobs they do. When Jesus lived on earth as a man he thought that everyone was important. He had time for rich people and poor, for people who were ill and those who were well, for the old and young, for those with jobs and those that begged on the streets. Everyone mattered to Jesus.

Story

Go on to tell short narratives from the gospels which illustrate this, for example:

Jesus had time for everyone. He had meals with rich people like Zacchaeus, the tax collector, who was rich because he cheated people. Jesus went to his house and, because Jesus became his friend, Zacchaeus gave away the money he had stolen.

But Jesus also saw a very poor lady put all the money that she had in an offering box at the temple, and he praised her for doing that. Jesus spent a lot of time making ill people better, like the man whose hand wouldn't work, or people who were blind. But he also spent a lot of time listening and talking with people about God, like the 5,000 people who went to hear him one day.

Jesus helped an old lady who was his friend's mother, when she was ill, and he did the same for a twelve-year-old girl who was dying, when her father came to ask for help.

Jesus talked to people as they were working, like Peter and Andrew the fishermen, and he stopped to talk to people who had no job, like Bartimaeus, who was blind and had to beg for money.

Everyone mattered to Jesus!

Application

Tell the children that today, everyone still matters to Jesus. Jesus cares about each and every one of us here, and about each and every person in the world.

Time to reflect

1   Encourage the children to be still and close their eyes.

2   Ask them to think about how each person is important to Jesus, no matter what age they are, how they look, what they can or can't do.

Prayer

Invite the children to join in the following prayer or a similar one by saying 'Amen' at the end:

Dear Jesus, thank you that you had time for everyone, for poor and rich, for sick and well, for young and old alike. Thank you too that we all matter to you today and that you love each and every one of us. Amen.

Song suggestion

• Everyone in the whole wide world, 333, *Junior Praise*

9   I'M ME!

Aim: To help the children understand that God knows all about us, even the things that make us unique individuals. He made us special.

Bible base: Luke 15; Psalm 139

You will need:

- A simple sheep puppet of some kind eg a sock puppet, a paper bag puppet, a wooden spoon puppet

Preparation

- Prepare or obtain your sheep puppet.
- Learn the story and practise telling it using the puppet.

Presentation

Introduction
1   Ask the children if they have ever been lost. How did it happen? How did they feel? How were they found?
2   Tell the children that you know a sheep that got lost. Introduce your puppet and tell the sheep's story.

Story
Idris the sheep lives on a farm under the shadow of the great mountain Cader Idris in North Wales, after which he is named. He is well looked after by Mr Williams, the shepherd, who makes sure that all the sheep in the flock are well fed and cared for.

Mr Williams knows everything about each one of the sheep – its name, its special favourite places to eat grass, how they lie when they sleep at night and probably even what each sheep is thinking! Imagine that! With Idris, that's not too difficult. He's always dreaming of the great mountain with which he shares a name, and of what it would be like to climb up to the very top and look out over the deep blue sea.

Well one day Idris got his chance! A boy from the farm came running to fetch Mr Williams to help a ewe give birth to triplet lambs. In the short time that Mr Williams' back was turned and the gate was open, Idris escaped for his adventure!

Idris ran up the next field and wriggled under a gate that was a bit broken. It was quite a climb up the hill but he was fairly fit and very determined. As he climbed higher and higher the farm looked smaller and smaller, until Idris forgot all about the rest of the sheep and Mr Williams the shepherd. Until, that is, it began to go dark. Idris shivered a bit as the sun went down and shadows from the moonlight began to stretch out across the mountain. He was cold, he was still a long way from the top, and he was beginning to feel a bit frightened.

Stumbling up the mountain, Idris took his eyes off the path for a moment and suddenly felt himself falling! There was nothing he could do until he landed with a hard bump on some very rocky ground. Idris tried hard to get up but – oh no! He had hurt his foot as he fell. He began to cry, but there was no one to hear his bleating. Poor Idris!

Mr Williams the shepherd went back to his sheep when the triplet lambs had been born and were safely tucked up in their pen. Everything looked all right, but he thought he had better check. He counted the sheep by number and by name. 'Rosie, Penny, Dewi, Gwyn...' until he reached Idris' name in his head. Where was Idris? Certainly not in the field. But do you remember what I said earlier, that Mr Williams even knew what each sheep was thinking? He guessed straight away where Idris would be, for he knew all about the little sheep's fascination with the great mountain of the same name. So, closing the gate firmly to keep the other sheep in, Mr Williams set off up the mountain.

Mr Williams didn't daydream like Idris: he watched carefully where he put his feet. He had a powerful torch to see the way in the dark and, keeping to well-worn paths, Mr Williams climbed Cader Idris, calling all the time for the sheep of the same name. I think you can guess what happened!

Mr Williams found Idris and climbed down to rescue him. He tucked the sheep inside his coat, for Idris was still quite small, and carried him safely home. The next day he asked the vet to come and Idris had a special splint put on his broken foot. Idris the sheep never again tried to escape to the top of the mountain called by the same name.

Application

1   Tell the children that just as the shepherd knew all about Idris in our story, even what he was thinking, God knows about each one of us. He cares for us too, like the shepherd cares for the sheep.

2   God knows the things that are special just to you, the things that make you different from anyone else – *your* favourite toy, *your* favourite place to go, *your* friends.

3   Make the point that there is something different about each of us. Even identical twins don't have the same fingerprints and are different in other ways too. God knows every part of us and loves us just the way we are.

Prayer

Thank you, God, that you have made us all different. Thank you that each one of us is special to you.

Song suggestion

- There is no one else like you, 476, *Junior Praise*
- A wiggly waggly worm, 306, *Junior Praise*
- God made furry things, 65, *Big Blue Planet*

10 EVEN THOUGH I'M NAUGHTY

Aim: To help the children understand that they still remain special to God when they do wrong things, even though those things hurt God and make him sad.

Bible base: Luke 19:1–9

You will need:

- A copy of one of the 'My naughty little sister' books
- Three large flashcards with the words 'Hooray!', 'That's me!' and 'Lovely'

Presentation

Introduction

1   Ask the children if they know any of the 'My naughty little sister' stories. Which ones? What happens? Allow the children time to respond.

2   Find a suitable short extract to read.

3   Discuss some of the naughty things she gets up to.

4   Lead into the story by saying that today they will hear about Zacchaeus, someone Jesus met who cheated and stole from people. Because of this he didn't have any friends.

Story

Use three volunteers to hold up your cards for the rest of the children to see and respond whenever you say the following words:

Jesus   – 'Hooray' card – *(punch air with fist)*
Zacchaeus – 'That's me' card – *(raise one finger)*
money – 'Lovely' card – *(rub hands together)*

Explain to everyone that they can help with the story by joining in with the responses and actions whenever the appropriate words are mentioned. Have a little practice.

There was once a man called **Zacchaeus**, but most people called him Shortie in an unkind way, as he really wasn't very tall. There was one thing that **Zacchaeus** wasn't short of and that was **money**. You see, **Zacchaeus** was a tax collector, that meant he had to get money from everyone and give it to the people in charge of the country at that time. But **Zacchaeus** was greedy and he asked for more money than he should have done and kept the extra for himself! Most people knew that **Zacchaeus** cheated them and didn't want to be his friend, so he was very lonely.

One day **Zacchaeus** heard people talking about a special visitor who was on his way to town. They called the man **Jesus** and people said he was something very special and that he could do amazing things. **Zacchaeus** got all excited. He wanted to see this man for himself, so off he ran to catch up with the crowds who had set out to meet him. Suddenly the crowds of people stopped and **Zacchaeus** realised **Jesus** was just ahead, but there was no way he could see over all those people. **Zacchaeus** spotted a tree and before too long had managed to struggle up onto a big branch from where he had a brilliant view.

Zacchaeus hadn't been up there very long when **Jesus** walked right under the tree and stopped!

'**Zacchaeus**, come down,' called **Jesus**. 'I want to visit your house and talk to you.' Well, **Zacchaeus** nearly fell out of that tree, but he was soon leading **Jesus** along the way to his house, as all the people stared at what was happening.

Jesus and **Zacchaeus** had a very long chat over tea. **Zacchaeus** couldn't believe how much **Jesus** seemed to know about him. He found himself telling **Jesus** all about the things he was doing wrong. After tea **Zacchaeus** did something which even surprised him. He ran outside to the waiting crowds and made an announcement. 'If I've cheated any of you I'm going to give you back four times as much as I owe, I'm so sorry.'

Zacchaeus was so different after that day. He gave half his belongings to the poor people and stopped stealing **money**. 'What a change in **Zacchaeus** there has been since he met **Jesus**,' everyone said.

Application

1   Ask the children in what way Zacchaeus changed. Ask them if they think it is hard or easy to stop doing wrong things.

2   Make the point that Jesus still visited Zacchaeus even though he was a cheat. He still had time for him and cared.

3   Remind the children that they are still special to God even though they do wrong things and that he can help them change like Zacchaeus did.

Prayer

Dear God, please forgive us when we do wrong things... when we tell lies, when we're rude and unkind, when we fight. Help us to live in a way that pleases you. Amen.

Song suggestion

*   Zacchaeus was a very little man, 300, *Junior Praise*
*   Who's that sitting in the sycamore tree?, 32, *Someone's singing Lord*

11 I'M WORTH IT

Aim: To help the children see that God thinks we are special –
so special he sent Jesus to die and rise again for us.

Bible base: Mark 14–16. The Easter story.

You will need:

- A chocolate egg
- A toy baby animal (a lamb, a chick etc)
- A sticky bun (a hot cross bun if possible)
- The shape of the cross (cut from paper or a wooden one)
- The words 'Empty' and 'Risen' written out on large flashcards
- Six cards with the letters **E A S T E R** written on them
- 'God thinks I'm worth it' on acetate or paper
- OHP if using acetate

Presentation

1 Choose six children to come and stand at the front to help you.
Ask the children what they look forward to at Easter time.

Is it the Easter eggs? (*Give one of the volunteers the egg to hold up
and so on with the following items.*)

Or maybe the signs of new life around them, the lambs and chicks?
Eating hot cross buns?

2 But Easter for Christians is all about Jesus. They remember how
Jesus died on a cross. (*Reveal your paper cross and pass it to one of
your volunteers.*)

3 Jesus was so special that he didn't stay dead; when his friends
went to the cave where they had buried him it was empty. (*Child to
hold up 'Empty' card.*)

4 God's power had brought Jesus back to life, he had risen! (*Last
child to hold 'Risen' card.*)

5 Go to each volunteer in turn and replace their item or word with
a letter card explaining as you go through:

E – for Easter egg
A – for animal
S – for sticky bun
T – stands for the shape of the cross
E – for 'empty'
R – for 'risen'

Application
1   Talk to the children about how much God must love us if he was prepared to send his son Jesus to die for us.
2   We are worth so much to God – we are all precious to him.

Time to reflect

1   Put up the words 'God thinks I'm worth it' on a slide on the OHP or on some paper. Make the three 't's cross shapes.
2   Read the words with the children and ask them to think about them quietly for a few moments.
3   Draw their attention to the crosses and remind the children that they are so special Jesus died for them.

Prayer

Dear God, thank you that your love for us is so big. Thank you that you never stop loving us. Amen.

Song suggestions

* I'm special because God has loved me, 106, *Junior Praise*
* When I think about the cross, 99, *Everybody Praise*

12 I CAN DO IT

Aim: To show the children that we can all do something for God. He takes what we offer and makes it something special for him.

Bible base: John 6:1–14

You will need:

- A piece of artwork, a football, a piece of maths work, a sweeping brush, a smiling face drawn on a paper plate, some dancing shoes (anything that shows achievements of the children, including cleaning up well or cheering someone up)
- Some volunteers to mime
- A few simple props – five rolls and two fish (cut from card) packed in a small basket/box etc

Preparation

Study the script and the Bible passage to familiarise yourself with the story.

Presentation

Introduction

1   Talk to the children about the things they enjoy doing or things that they are particularly good at.

2   Use your items to illustrate different skills, pointing out that some of us are particularly good at helping others, being kind or friendly, cleaning up, cheering people etc. All these things are important.

3   Ask for six volunteers to come out and help you tell the story by miming the parts: Peter, Thomas, Jesus, Philip, Andrew, boy. The rest of the children are the crowd.

Story

FAST FOOD FOR FIVE THOUSAND
It had been a hot day.
Everyone was warm and sweaty and hungry.

The crowds had been with Jesus all day, listening to him.

They were sitting on grass, on stones, under trees, up trees and in some cases on thistles (ouch!) and they didn't mind.

They felt as though they could listen to what Jesus was saying and never have enough.

When it was almost sunset, the disciples thought the people would go back home... but they didn't.

'Those children ought to be in bed,' said Peter.

(*Peter wags his finger at the crowd as this is said.*)

'Those women should be cooking their husbands' suppers,' said Thomas. (*Thomas also wags his finger at the crowd.*)

A lady who was standing nearby knocked him on the head with her basket. 'My husband is quite capable of cooking his own supper,' she said.

There was a distant rumbling sound. Was it thunder? Peter patted his tummy.

'Sorry,' he said, 'I always rumble when I'm hungry.' (*Peter rubs his tummy.*)

The other disciples laughed, but the thought of supper was making them all ravenous.

As Jesus paused in speaking Philip tugged at his sleeve. (*Jesus and Philip to mime.*)

'It's sunset,' he said. 'Isn't it time you finished off, so the people can go?'

Jesus smiled. 'We're miles away from anywhere. What do you expect the people to do?'

'It's time for our tea,' said Philip. 'Peter's tummy sounds like a volcano. We need food and so do you and what about the people? They might be able to find food in the villages and farms. There might be a fast food place...' his voice trailed off hesitantly.

'Fast food for all this lot?' said Jesus, waving his arms over the crowd. 'Good idea. Can you find some?'

Philip and the others gulped.

For the first time they looked at how huge the crowd was.

Rows of people, groups of children and women and men, stretched away as far as they could see.

'What about it?' said Jesus.

Philip went pale. 'Have you any idea how much it would cost?' he said, his voice wobbling.

'A sandwich for everyone here would be hundreds of pounds, there must be over 5,000 people here!'

Andrew felt someone tugging at his sleeve. There was a very small boy. (*Andrew and boy to mime.*)

'Not now son,' said Andrew. 'We're having a crisis.'

He turned back to Jesus and Philip.

'What's that?' said the little boy.

'It's a grown-up word for a big problem.'

'Oh, sorry,' said the boy. 'I thought you might be hungry.'

Andrew bent down to him. He had a clean face but otherwise he was very dirty. He'd been sitting on the ground all day in the dusty heat.

'What have you got?' said Andrew.

'Two big fish – well, medium – and **five** rolls. I can't eat them all myself and Mum said to share.'

Andrew took him by the grubby hand and led him to Jesus.

'Hello,' said Jesus. 'Who are you?'

'He's a boy who wants to share,' said Andrew.

'Get everyone sitting down,' said Jesus.

While the disciples organised everyone, Jesus looked into the little boy's basket and saw the fish and the loaves.

'Father God,' prayed Jesus holding up the basket. 'Thank you for this food and for all you give us. Amen.'

'Amen,' said the boy.

'Would you like to help?' said Jesus. The boy nodded.

'I'll need some more baskets,' he called to the disciples.

They gathered some from the people, and Jesus started dividing out the bread and fish while the disciples and the boy took it to the different groups. Every time they went back for more they were sure there would not be any left. Every time there was more. How could it be happening?

Eventually everyone was fed and they began to clear up.

'How could there be any leftovers?' thought Philip.

But there were leftovers – twelve basketfuls!

'Wow,' said the boy, 'you're amazing, Jesus!'

Application

1   Make the point to the children that the boy did what he could – he offered his lunch to Jesus – and Jesus did something very special with it.

2   In the same way today, if we offer to Jesus the things we can do, he will use them.

Prayer

> Lord Jesus, thank you for all the things we can do... painting pictures, writing stories, dancing, making music, helping others. Please help us to do all these things for you. Amen.

Song suggestion

- A boy gave to Jesus, 1, *Junior Praise*

13 AS I GROW

Aim: To help the children understand that they remain special to God as they grow up and change.

Bible base: Mark 10:13–16; Luke 13:10–13

You will need:

- A picture of yourself as a baby
- A toy car and a set of car keys
- A babygrow suit and an adult-sized jumper
- A cloth or plastic baby book and a thick novel
- A Bible

Preparation

- Look up the two Bible passages – if possible look at them in a children's Bible or work out how to tell the stories simply in your own words.

Presentation

1   Show the children your baby picture and talk to them a little about what you were like.

2   Then discuss how you have changed – size, looks, etc.

3   Show them the toy car and say that as a baby you would have enjoyed having this but now you enjoy driving a real one! (*Show them the car keys.*)

4   Hold up the babygrow and then the jumper – talk about how you would never fit into the babygrow now but the jumper is just right.

5   Show the children the baby book and the novel, make comparisons and talk about why they are appropriate at the different stages.

6   Talk about how we all grow out of things. We change and different things happen to us. Remind them that God cares about us however old we are and whatever happens to us.

7   Tell the children the stories from the Bible which show us how Jesus had time for little children and for an old lady with a bent back. (*Use a children's Bible or just explain things simply.*)

Time to reflect

1   Ask the children to sit very still, close their eyes and to think about what they have heard in the assembly.

2   Remind them of how Jesus treated old and young alike – he had time for the children and time to make an old lady better.

3   As they grow up and things change they will always be special to God. He won't stop loving them.

Song suggestion

•   Everyone in the whole wide world, 333, *Junior Praise*

SECTION 3

A SPECIAL FRIEND

14 GOD ALWAYS WANTS TO HELP US

Aim: To help the children understand that we can ask God for help at any time. Also to show them that God is stronger than any bully and will always be with them.

Bible base: Exodus 7–11. The plagues on Egypt.

You will need:

- A few simple props for the first telling of the story, eg a stick, a red scarf, a toy frog etc
- A copy of the rap (included below)
- The chorus of the rap written out on acetate or on a large sheet of paper

Presentation

Introduction

1   Talk about anything that you have had to do, or a situation you have been in, that made you feel scared or in need of help.

2   Ask the children if they have ever had to do anything that has really scared them or ask them to tell you about a time when they needed some help.

Allow them time to respond.

3   Give a little background information on the story you will be telling the children, eg God's special people the Israelites were slaves in Egypt; God had chosen Moses to go to the Pharaoh (like the king) and tell him to let the people go.

Story

1   Choose some children to be actors, to act out the story (given below) of Moses going to Pharaoh and the plagues.

2   Talk about how the Pharaoh 'bullied' Moses.

3   Use your volunteer actors to move about and use the simple props as you tell the story:

Moses and his brother Aaron stood before the king of all Egypt, the Pharaoh.

God says, 'Let my people go!' they told him.

This didn't impress Pharaoh at all, in fact it made him very angry indeed. He gave orders that the Israelites, who were slaves in Egypt, should no longer be given straw to make bricks but should have to find it themselves. This was dreadful news and Moses and Aaron left at once.

Moses cried out to God in desperation and God answered him. He told Moses that he would show his power and make Pharaoh set the Israelites free. He told Moses to go back to Pharaoh and tell him that God would send great trouble if he didn't do as God had asked. So Moses and Aaron went back to Pharaoh and told him what God had said.

'Show me something that will prove God has sent you,' Pharaoh said.

Aaron threw down his stick and it became a snake. But the Egyptian magicians could do this too and Moses and Aaron were sent away.

God did what he had said. He sent great trouble on all Egypt. Dreadful things started to happen and after each one God warned Pharaoh to listen to him but he wouldn't.

First the water in the river Nile turned blood-red. Then frogs invaded Egypt; they were everywhere. Next swarms of insects and flies arrived and then the animals began to die.

The people then became covered in nasty boils and enormous hail stones fell from the sky.

Locusts came and ate up every green thing, and after that pitch darkness covered the land for three days. Still Pharaoh wouldn't let the people go.

Then the most dreadful thing of all happened. One night the eldest son in every Egyptian family died, even the Pharaoh's son.

Then the Israelites were allowed to leave Egypt. In fact the Egyptians couldn't wait for them to leave!

4 Tell the children that you know a rap of the story too. Encourage them to join in clapping with two fingers on every second beat and to say the words at each chorus. Warn them that the last chorus is different.

EGYPTIAN RAP

Lord God sent Moses to Pharaoh one day,
To ask that king to let His people go away,
Gave Aaron power with a special stick,
But Pharaoh said, 'Anyone can do that trick!'

Chorus
So, Pharaoh said, 'No,'
Yes, Pharaoh said, 'No,'
Yes, Pharaoh said, 'No, no, no, no, no!'

Lord God changed the river from water to blood,
The frogs jumped out and they landed thud,
They came in the houses, they jumped in the streets,
The people found them in their beds and under their sheets.

Chorus

Then gnats and flies came buzzing round,
Every room was filled with a ghastly sound,
The people scratched, and the people cried,
When one day they found that all the animals had died.

Chorus

Then boils popped up all over their skin,
Didn't matter if they were fat or thin,
The hail beat down and the locusts came,
But still old Pharaoh said just the same.

Chorus

Then God sent darkness all over the land,
You couldn't see the sky and you couldn't see your hand,
An angel came down and the first born died,
All over the land the Egyptians cried.

Chorus

Then Pharaoh said, 'Go,'
Yes, Pharaoh said, 'Go,'
Yes, Pharaoh said, 'Go, go, go, go, go!'

Application
1 Talk to the children about God's presence with Moses when Pharaoh was bullying him and how God helped Moses.
2 Make the point that God is with us all the time.
He is bigger and stronger than any bully and we can always ask him to help us.

Prayer

Thank you, God, that you are stronger than any bully. Please help us to remember this when we are scared.
Thank you that you have promised to be with us always. Amen.

Song suggestions

- My God is so big, 169, *Junior Praise*
- When Israel was in Egypt's land, 276, *Junior Praise*

15 GOD ALWAYS FORGIVES

Aim: To show the children that God loves us and forgives us when we say sorry.

Bible base: Luke 15:11–32. The Lost Son.

You will need:

- Three paper plates – one with a happy face, one with a sad face, one with a face with a jealous expression
- Three flash cards with the following wording:

  1 Dig, dig,
  Work, work,
  Sweat, sweat,
  Phew!

2   Get, get,
    Money, money,
    Spend, spend,
    Gone!

3   Love, love,
    Love, love,
    Love, love,
    Love!

Preparation

- If possible read the story from a modern translation of the Bible.
- Make the flash cards.

Presentation

Introduction

1   Show the children the faces on the plates and talk about times they have felt happy, sad or jealous over something.

2   Ask them to listen carefully to the story for times when people had these feelings.

Story

Choose three pairs of children to hold the flash cards. The younger children will not be able to read these words, but they will remind the older children of what to say. Practise the sayings, and teach the children the following actions for the last line of each:

– wipe the back of your hand over your forehead for 'phew!'

– hold out both hands, palms up, to signify 'gone!'

– hug yourself for 'love!'

Some people were grumbling about the kind of people Jesus spent time with. Jesus mixed with people that no one else would speak to! So one day Jesus told them a story.

There was once a man who had two sons. The older one stayed at home and worked very hard for his father.
Card 1

The younger one wanted to go off and to see the world, so one day he went to his dad and asked for his share of the money that one day would be his.
Card 2

The father thought for a while about how much he loved his son.
Card 3

And somewhat sadly he said, 'Yes, son' and gave the boy his share.

So when the money had been collected together for him, the boy left home and went off to a faraway country. (*Take the children with this card round to the back of the room, as if going on a journey. Ask the children for ideas of how he might have spent his money.*)

For a while he had lots of fun spending the money, buying whatever he wanted, spending the money on new clothes and eating the best food, on having parties and buying things for the new friends he had made. Until one day, the money ran out.
Card 2

So the young man had to get a job, and he found one on a farm, feeding the pigs. After a while in that country there wasn't enough food for everyone, and the young man became very, very hungry. He was so hungry that he felt like eating the pigs' food! You know when there are leftovers from dinners at school? They get put in a bucket and given to feed pigs. Just imagine it! The boy was so hungry that he would have eaten leftover baked beans and chocolate pudding and chips and pizza and yoghurt all thrown in together! Then he suddenly realised how stupid he had been.

'Back home, even the servants on my dad's farm have better food than this. They have three good meals a day and a warm bed to sleep in. I wonder if my father would ever take me back to be one of his servants if I went to him and said "sorry" for what I have done?'

So the young man decided to go back home.

When he was still some distance from the house, his father saw him and ran to meet him. The young man knelt down at his father's feet and began to speak. 'I'm sorry for what I have done wrong. I'm not fit to be your son. Will you let me come back as one of your servants?'

But before he had finished speaking, his dad hugged him.
Card 3

He shouted for people to bring his best clothes for his son to wear; to bring shoes for his feet and a ring for his finger, and to get food ready for a party! The dad loved his son so much that he forgave him everything.
Card 3

When the older son heard this he was very cross. 'It's not fair!' he said. 'I've stayed at home and worked hard all this time.
Card 1

'You never gave me a party!'

'I know,' said his father, "and you know that I love you very much."
Card 3

'But your brother was lost and he is found, so we had to have a party, because I love him very much too.'
Card 3

Application
- Talk about the happy, sad and jealous feelings in the story.
    - a) to begin with the money made the younger son happy – the father was extremely happy when his son came home.
    - b) the younger son made his father sad by going away – the older son made him sad by being cross when his brother returned.
    - c) the older brother was jealous at the way his father treated his younger brother.
- There are things that we do that hurt other people and hurt God.
- God is like the dad in the story. He forgives us when we say 'sorry' and always keeps on loving us.

Prayer

Use the following prayer or similar:

Dear God, we are sorry for hurting other people and you by the wrong things that we do. Please forgive us and help us to do the things that please you. Amen.

Song suggestions
- Father, 13, *Everybody Praise*
- Sometimes I'm naughty, 460, *Junior Praise*

16 GOD ALWAYS ANSWERS

Aim: To show the children that prayer is answered.

Bible base: Acts 12:1–11. Peter is set free from prison.

You will need:

- 'Doors' visual aid, as illustrated on pages 68–69

Preparation

- Make the visual aid by photocopying the pictures on to A4 thin card or, if possible, enlarging them to A3 size.
- Cut the doors on illustrations 1–3 so they open. Then stick all the pictures on top of each other starting with the picture of Rhoda at the bottom, then the three doors in order of size so the largest door is on the top.
- Have all the doors closed to begin with, so you can open them one by one as you tell the story.
- You may like to colour the illustrations.

Presentation

Introduction

- Begin by asking the children who helps them when they are lonely, frightened or worried?
- Do they talk to anyone about their fears?

Story

1 Ask the children to help you tell a story about some people who talked to God when they needed help.

2 Whenever you say 'pray, prayed, praying or prayer' they are to say, 'Hello Lord'.

3 As you tell the story use the 'Doors' visual aid to show Peter's escape, and allow the children time to join in the response 'Hello Lord' but not waiting for them if they get too caught up in the story!

> Peter hung his head and tried to get some sleep. It wasn't easy to sleep sitting between two soldiers with both hands chained. He knew his friends were praying (*'Hello Lord'*) for him but what could

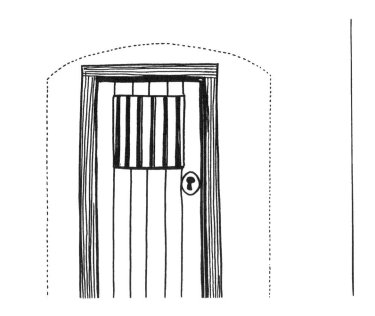

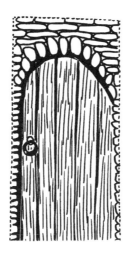

God do now. Suddenly, just when Peter had managed to doze off, he felt someone shaking him. 'Get up Peter. Fasten your belt, put your cloak and shoes on and follow me.' There before him stood an angel! Peter thought he was dreaming!

Then another strange thing happened. As Peter followed the angel they walked straight past the soldiers on guard and the cell door just opened in front of them. (*Open first door of visual aid.*) Then the same thing happened as they reached the very outer door of the prison itself. (*Open next door.*) and Peter found himself out on the street. He looked round and the angel had disappeared!

Peter's first thoughts were of his friends praying for him. (*'Hello Lord'*) He set off into the darkness to find Mary's house where they usually met. When he reached the house he knocked at the door and waited. Eventually a servant girl named Rhoda peered cautiously round the door, (*Begin to open the last door of your visual aid.*) 'Who is it?' she whispered. 'It's me, Peter, let me in,' came the reply. 'But Peter's in prison, that's why we're all here praying for him,' (*'Hello Lord'*) said Rhoda. 'But God's answered your prayers (*'Hello Lord'*). He sent an angel to help me escape,' explained Peter.

'That's wonderful,' said Rhoda, and before Peter could get inside she'd shut the door and run upstairs to tell everyone the news. Poor Peter had to go on knocking until someone actually believed Rhoda and she came downstairs again to let Peter in! (*Open last door fully to reveal Rhoda.*) Everyone listened carefully to Peter's story and then they thanked God for answering their prayers (*'Hello Lord'*) in such a wonderful way.

Application

1   Ask the children what they think Peter's friends might have asked God to do for him.

2   Sometimes God does far more than we can ever imagine, and answers our prayers in amazing ways.

3   Sometimes God says 'no' to what we ask him for. We may not understand why; we have to trust that he knows what is best.

4   One thing we can be sure about is that God always hears our prayers and answers them, even if the answer is 'no' or 'not yet.'

Prayer

After this story it may be appropriate to ask the children to think of something specific that they can ask God about – either for themselves or something that is topical locally or at national news level.

Song Suggestion

- Did you ever talk to God above?, 329, *Junior Praise*
- God has made me and he knows me, 346, *Junior Praise*

17 JESUS CAN DO ANYTHING – TRUST HIM.

Aim: To show the children that Jesus has the power to do anything and that he will never let us down.

Bible base: Matthew 14:22–32. Jesus walks on the water.

You will need:

- The letters **I M P O S S I B L E** written out individually on pieces of A4 paper big enough for everyone to see
- A set of quiz questions
- Some paper with two cuts down the middle
- A short message written out and something to attach it to a child's back with – tape, safety pin etc

Presentation

Introduction

1 Use the following quiz to introduce the assembly. Play the quiz by asking the children to guess the one word answer to the following questions. You take the first letter of the word and ask the child who guessed it correctly to hold it up at the front.

Letter Quiz

1	I	Opposite of out (In)
2	M	It helps you when you are lost (Map)
3	P	They catch bad people (Police)
4	O	Noise a pig makes (Oink)
5	S	Round and hot and we get light from it (Sun)
6	S	First day of the week (Sunday)
7	I	An Eskimo's home (Igloo)
8	B	We learn about God from this book (Bible)
9	L	A baby sheep (Lamb)
10	E	A chick hatches out of it (Egg)

Read together the word you have made.

2   Impossible Challenges

Talk about how some things are just impossible to do. Try these as examples…

(*Ask for three volunteers and see if they can do the following*)

* Tear paper with two cuts down the middle, holding the sides only.
* Read a message attached to their back.
* Lift yourself up.

Tell the children that you are going to tell a story of a time when Jesus did something impossible.

3   Tell the story below, encouraging everyone to join in with some sound effects.

Practise the sound effects before you start.

Story

Jesus had been teaching the people for a long time. He told his disciples to go to the other side of the lake in a boat.

boat leaves (SWOOSH)

Jesus goes off to pray.

It is late at night and on the boat some are sleeping and some are keeping watch.

people sleeping (ZZZZZZ)

One man on watch sees someone walking on the water.

looking at someone walking on the water (AAAARGH – IT'S A GHOST!)

But it was Jesus and he said, 'Don't be afraid – it's me.'

When they realised it was Jesus they began to relax.
Peter who was feeling a bit brave said, 'Let me come out to you.'
'All right,' said Jesus, 'come and walk to me.'
> *Peter walking on the water (WOW)*

Peter was not too far from Jesus when he took his eyes off Jesus and began to sink.
> *Peter sinking (OH NO)*

Jesus reached out and pulled Peter out of the water.
> *Peter being pulled out of the water (SSSH WEEE POP)*
> *Relief (PHEW)*

Jesus said, 'How little faith you have!'
I think Peter forgot to trust Jesus who can do anything.

Application
Talk about:
1 How Jesus can do the impossible – because of who he is – God's Son.
2 How he is able to help us.
3 How even though our best friend, parents, teachers may sometimes let us down, Jesus never will.
4 How we need to rely on him.

Conclusion
1 Invite the same three children you involved earlier to come out.
2 This time when they try to rip the paper, read what is on their back or lift themselves up, you can help them. Making the impossible possible.
3 Draw the parallel that if we ask Jesus he will help us make the impossible possible. It would also be important to mention that this does not mean when things get tough Jesus will take our problems away, but rather that he will help us in them.

Prayer
> *Dear God thank you that you can do impossible things. Help us to remember that you are always there to help us.*

Song suggestion
- With Jesus in the boat you can smile at the storm, 291, *Junior Praise*
- One day when we were fishing, 18, *Big Blue Planet*

18 JESUS ALWAYS LISTENS

Aim: To help the children understand that Jesus listens when they talk to him. He is happy to hear their prayers.

Bible base: John 3:1–21. Jesus and Nicodemus.

You will need:

- A collection of objects that make some kind of a noise, eg a cup and saucer, an alarm clock, an egg timer (wind up kind), a hand bell, a radio, etc (try to include the radio or something else with words – a cassette player, a talking toy!)
- A deep box for your objects, with a hole made in one side, large enough for your hands to go through

Presentation

Introduction

1   Start the assembly with a listening game.
- Ask the children to listen very carefully to the things in your box, ensuring that they cannot see over the top into the box.
- Put your hands into the back of the box through the hole. Make a noise with each object in turn.
- As the children guess the objects correctly take them out of the box. Leave your 'speaking' object until last. See if the children can actually make out some of the words being said.

2   Talk to the children about whether they are good or bad listeners. There are times when it is important to listen. Talk about what it feels like when people don't listen to you properly or at all.

Story

THE SECRET VISITOR:

We read in the Bible about a time when a man came to Jesus wanting Jesus to listen to his questions and to answer them.

Tell the story of Nicodemus coming to Jesus by night (given below). Emphasise how much Nicodemus wanted to talk to Jesus and how willing Jesus was to listen.

Nicodemus was a teacher. He had heard a lot about Jesus, and wanted to talk to him. But he didn't want people to see him – so he came after dark.

'We know you've been sent by God,' Nicodemus began. 'No one could do the wonderful things you do without God's help.'

Jesus knew the questions in Nicodemus' mind.

'You are a great teacher,' Jesus said. 'But you still have lessons to learn. You want to please God. But being good isn't enough. You must be born all over again to enjoy God's kingdom.'

'What do you mean?' Nicodemus asked.

'You need a fresh start, a whole new life,' Jesus answered, 'the life I have come to bring. You see, God loves the world so much that he has sent his Son. Everyone who puts his trust in me can have this new kind of life.'

Outside it was dark. Inside the house, the lamp shone.

'God's light is shining in the world,' Jesus said.

'But people would rather live in the dark because the light shows up the wrong they do.'

[Story from 'The Lion Children's Bible', retold by Pat Alexander. Used with permission.]

Application

1   Ask the children how Nicodemus must have felt as Jesus sat and listened to him.

2   Remind them that Jesus still listens when we talk to him in our prayers. He is so wonderful, he knows what each person has said even if they say it at the same time. He listens wherever we are and always answers us.

Song suggestion

•   Prayer is like a telephone, 448, *Junior Praise*

19 JESUS IS ALWAYS THERE

Aim: To help the children understand that Jesus has promised to be with them always, wherever they are.

Bible base: Matthew 28:16–20 and Acts 1:1–9. Jesus goes back to heaven.

You will need:

- A 'Forever Friends' card
- A lollipop head puppet

Preparation

- Ask someone to write you a card from the 'Forever Friends' range that says 'goodbye' to you because they are leaving the area.
- Make your lollipop head puppet. Make two circles of card, one with a smiling face on a yellow background, the other with a sad face on a blue background. Stick the two circles back to back placing a lolly stick or another kind of stick between them.

Presentation

Introduction

1   Show the children the card and draw their attention to the fact that it is from the 'Forever Friends' range.

2   Talk about your feelings over your friend leaving. Include the fact that you can keep in touch by letter or phone, even though you may not see each other again.

3   Ask the children if any of them have had to say goodbye to a friend and talk about the feelings they had. Link this with the disciples' feelings as they met to say goodbye to Jesus.

Story

Tell the story of the ascension (a simple version is given below) using the lollipop head puppet to show the sad feelings of the disciples as Jesus left them and the happy ones at Jesus' promise to be with them all for ever by his Spirit.

Jesus and his friends had all gone to a place called the Mount of Olives. It was about six weeks since Jesus had come alive again from the dead and now they were together to say their last goodbyes to Jesus. They all felt very sad. (*Show sad face of puppet.*)

Jesus began to tell them something very special and exciting. He promised them that soon God would send them a helper, his Spirit. God's Spirit would help them to be brave to tell other people what Jesus had said and done. They were to tell the whole world! His friends felt a bit happier at this news. (*Show happy face.*)

After Jesus had finished speaking he was taken up to heaven. As his friends watched a cloud hid him from them. Then all of a sudden two men all dressed in white were standing by them telling them that Jesus had gone back to heaven to be with God but one day he would come back!

(*Use happy and sad side – discuss how they would have felt as they watched Jesus go and listened to what they were told.*)

Application

1   The disciples realised that after Jesus had gone back to be with God they could no longer see, hear or touch him. But Jesus had promised that he would be with them always.

2   In the same way we cannot see Jesus now with our eyes, but he is with us by his Holy Spirit.

3   When we ask Jesus to be our friend he is a 'Forever Friend', with us not just now but always.

Song Suggestion

•   Jesus, Jesus, here I am, 20, *Spring Harvest Kids Praise 1988/9*

SECTION 4

A SPECIAL BOOK

These assemblies could be used individually, but they also follow a logical progression and work well as a series. The first introduces the theme, the fifth is a reminder of the intermediate three and the sixth explains what we should do about the Bible when we have read it.

20 BOOKSHELF

Aim: To explain to the children some of what the Bible contains.

Bible base: The Bible

You will need:

- Three sets of 'sandwich-boards' drawn to look like a Bible, a road atlas and a book of fairy stories
- Three adults to read these different parts, plus a leader

Preparation

- Make the sandwich-boards from cardboard so that they fit over the shoulders of the wearers.

Presentation

Story

'Bible' should stand in the centre. 'Road Atlas' enters, making car noises, and bumps into Bible.

BIBLE: Ouch! That was a nasty bump. Who are you? What are you doing on this shelf?

ROAD ATLAS: I'm a Road Atlas – can't you tell? *(more car noises)* I'm very important – you'd be lost without me. My maps can get you anywhere you want to go, *(names some local places of interest)*. I can take you to see your Granny if she lives a long way away; I can get you to places at the other end of the country. Don't ever set off on a journey without me! AND I'm on special offer at WH Smith's this week. So there! *(Exits.)*

BIBLE: Sounds interesting, but I've got maps in me too, although not of this country – they're of somewhere a long way away, but very special. Now who is this coming along the shelf?

(Enter Fairy Stories.)

FAIRY STORIES: *(reading Bible's cover)* The Bible... I guess you've not been read for a long time! I'm out every bedtime – I'm their favourite book! I'm full of adventures – The Little Mermaid, The Tin Soldier, The Ugly Duckling, The Emperor's New Clothes... exciting stories about important people and important things. AND I'm full of pictures! (*Exits.*)

BIBLE: I didn't like to interrupt, but I'm full of stories too – only mine are true! They are exciting stories, full of adventure, about special people and important things. Other books come and go, but I've been around a lot longer than those two. In fact I've sold more copies than any other book that has ever been written. God helped lots of different people to write me, and they all tell the most important story ever: that God loves people very much. Look – someone's come to read me! (*Exits.*)

Application

LEADER: The Bible is a very special book from God, just as we heard. It has lots of different sorts of stories in it.

Who has got a Bible at home? Who has read the Bible? Which stories do you know that are in the Bible?

Show where in the Bible are some of the stories that they mention, or some very well known ones, eg Noah in Genesis 6–9; David and Goliath in 1 Samuel 17; Jesus' birth in Luke 2; the lost sheep in Luke 15.

You may want to use a children's Bible that includes colour drawings.

Prayer

Thank you, God, for all the different stories in the Bible and for all the things that they tell us about you.

Song suggestion

- God loves you so much, 349, *Junior Praise*

21 LOOK HERE!

Aim: To show how the Bible is like a lamp.

Bible base: Psalm 119:105

You will need:
- A pen torch
- A picture/model of a lighthouse
- A large torch
- A night light or low wattage lamp
- A bright light to represent a spotlight
- An extension reel so that you can plug the lights in easily

Presentation

Show the lights one at a time and explain their use. Ask the children to say with you the word or sound (shown in bold type) that reminds us of the light's use, but to do so only once (or it could get out of hand!).

1   Pen torch
    Used by a doctor, to look down the throat.
    Looking into someone's throat can show up trouble. Dentists use little torches too, to show up trouble when a tooth needs filling. When they have seen a problem, both the doctor and the dentist do something to make it better.
    'Aaah.'
2   Lighthouse
    Shows up danger by flashing to warn ships of dangerous rocks. Without a lighthouse, the captain of the ship wouldn't see the rocks and might crash onto them and the ship might be wrecked.
    'Help!'
3   Large torch
    If you go to the cinema or theatre, people who work there sometimes have torches to show you the way to your seat when the place is dark. Without their help you might trip over, or go to the wrong seat, or even sit on someone's ice cream!
    'Ouch!'

4   Night light
Some people don't like sleeping without a bit of light in their room at night (tell the children if that was so for you). A night light (what I used to have!) or low-light (the modern equivalent) is comforting and helps if you are afraid in the dark.
'Oh dear!'
5   Spotlight
Used to show up something that is very special or important – eg at the theatre, to shine on an important actor.
'Ooh!'

Application

All these lights are there to help us in one way or another. The Bible is like a light: it actually says that in the Bible.

'Your word is a lamp to guide me and a light for my path.' Psalm 119:105.

1   The Bible shows up trouble and warns of danger (like the pen torch and lighthouse) because it tells us what is right and what is wrong.

2   It shows us the way to know God (like the usherette's torch).

3   It tells us about Jesus, the Light of the World, who is so very, very special (like the spotlight) and who will always be with us if we ask him, especially if we are afraid (like the low-light).

Prayer

End with a prayer saying thank you for all the different kinds of light that help us day by day, for the Bible that tells us more about God, and for Jesus who is the Light of the World.

Song suggestions

*   I am the light, the light of the world, 34, *Everybody Praise*
*   Father, Your Word is like a light in the darkness, 338, *Junior Praise*

22 LIBRARY BOOK

Aim: To explain what sort of books make up the Bible.

Bible base: The Bible

You will need:

- A selection of different types of books that children might read – poetry, how-to-do something, fiction, true stories, history, biography, scary stories, books about other places, funny stories, information books and animal books – ie as wide a range as possible. (Where possible, use topic or story books from school with which the children will be familiar.)
- Drawing of Bible books

Preparation

- Enlarge the drawing of the separate books of the Bible and colour code the different types of books.

Presentation

1   Ask the children if they like books and which books are their favourites. Give a couple the opportunity to say why, if they know.
2   Show the different types of books. Say a little about each as you do so – perhaps why you like it.
3   What is the name of the place where lots of different books are kept? The Bible is like a library with many different types of books in it.
4   Show the picture. There are:
- adventure stories (eg Daniel in the lions' den, Daniel 6:16–20)
- funny stories (eg Zacchaeus, Luke 19:1–4)
- the lives of kings and queens and ordinary people (Esther 5:1–2; Mark 1:16–18)
- poems and songs (Psalm 134)
- sad stories (2 Kings 2:11–12)
- happy ones (Luke 15:8–10)
- lots of things about how people lived, and lots more besides.

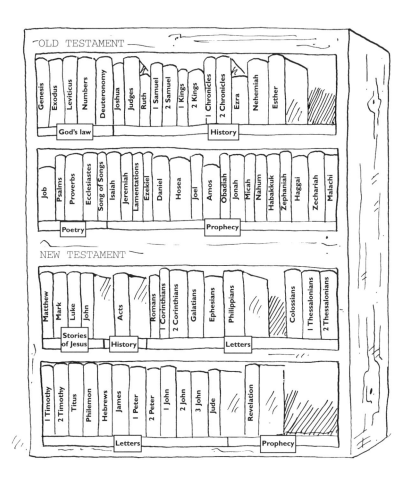

Application

1 The Bible is a special book for Christians because it tells people about God.

2 It's different from other books: you don't always start at page 1 when reading the Bible. People usually read a little bit at a time. But just as you might read a favourite story over and over again, people go back to parts of the Bible that are special to them and read them often.

3 If there are parts of the Bible that have been helpful or special to you at particular times, read a bit out and talk about it.

Prayer

Ask the children for more of their favourite books, and thank God for all of these.

Thank you, God, for giving us books to read and to enjoy. Thank you especially for these books that we have talked about, and for your special book, the Bible.

Song suggestion

- God loves you so much, 349, *Junior Praise*

23 WITH LOVE FROM ME TO YOU

Aim: To show the children that from the Bible we learn about God's love and care for us.

Bible base: The Bible

You will need:

- An assortment of letters
  - from family or friends, expressing love and care
  - something that is good news
  - directions to get somewhere
- A Bible in an envelope, addressed to the school and to 'everyone in the world'

Presentation

1   Talk generally about letters. Has the postman been to anyone's house today? What sort of letters come to our homes? Open the letters and read each one aloud.
2   The Bible is like a letter to us from God.
- Explain how the first letter showed love and care from family or friends, and the Bible does that too. It tells us

how God loves us and wants to be our friend. He showed just how much he loved us by sending Jesus into the world.

- It is really good news that someone loves us so much – even better than the news in the second letter.
- It's also good news that the Bible gives us directions for how to live our lives for the best.

Application

1   The only way to find out what is in a letter is to open it and to read it. We need to open and to read the Bible to find out what is in it and what God's 'letter' to us is.

2   Open the envelope and the Bible and read out John 3:16. Put the emphasis on the fact that God loves each and every one of us – in fact, everyone in the whole world.

Prayer

Thank you, God, for the Bible's good news that you love us very much.

Song suggestion

God loves you so much, 349, *Junior Praise*

24 WHAT COULD IT BE?

Aim: To help children to understand that the Bible has one overall message which God wants us to grasp: that he loves us very much.

Bible base: The Bible

You will need:

- A lamp or torch
- A set of books from one series that are separate stories but together make up a larger story (eg *Alfie & Annie Rose*, or *Lucy and Tom*, by Shirley Hughes)

- A letter
- A Bible
- Other Bible-related books (eg children's Bible reading notes, a Bible commentary, a Bible dictionary with pictures, different translations of the Bible, Bibles in foreign languages, a Bible puzzle book, a tape of Bible readings, a video of a Bible story)
- A box to put these in or cloth to cover them

Preparation

- Wrap the lamp/torch, the set of books and the letter as separate parcels. Put them in the box and cover.

Presentation

1   Show the children the box. Who can guess what might be in it? The parcels contain clues.
2   Have different children feel each parcel. What do they think it might contain? Then unwrap the parcels.
3   If you have already used the 'lamp/library/letter' outlines, ask the children what they think will be in the box.
4   When the final parcel has been opened show the Bible.
5   If you used the earlier outlines, remind them, or if not, tell them for the first time that the Bible says:
    - it is like a lamp because it shows us the way to God and the way we should live;
    - it is like a library because it is lots of individual stories that together make up one whole story;
    - it is like a letter because it is from God to us.

Application

1   Go on to show the translations, dictionaries etc that have been written to help us to read and to understand the Bible.
2   Although it looks very long and quite hard to read, the Bible tells us the same news all the way through, but in different ways: that God loves us very much and wants to be our friend.

Prayer

Thank you, God, for your love for us, and for the Bible that tells us lots of things about you. Please help us to understand it.

Song suggestions

God loves you so much, 349, *Junior Praise*
The baked bean song, 390, *Junior Praise*

25 TWO BUILDERS

Aim: As well as reading it, we need to do what the Bible tells us.

Bible base: Matthew 7:24–27. The two house-builders.

You will need:

- Some signs giving orders , eg 'Don't touch – hot' or 'Wait for the green man before crossing the road' etc
- Two hard hats, such as builders wear
- Two cheap, identical umbrellas
- A mist spray bottle, as used for spraying plants
- You may also want some kitchen roll to mop up the floor or even a paddling pool for the children to stand in! (But this would be more for effect: they shouldn't get that wet!)
- OHP if using acetates

Preparation

- Make the signs as above or write them on acetates.
- Make a number of holes in one of the umbrellas in such a way that they are not visible until it is opened.

Presentation

Introduction

1 Show the signs. What would happen if someone read them but then ignored them?
2 If you have previously used the assembly about the Bible as a letter, remind the children of the teaching point of the need to open it and to read it. If you have not used it, simply make that point now.
3 Jesus said that people should not just read the Bible but also should do what it says.

Story

1   Read the story of the two house-builders from the Bible. Re-tell the story simply, with two children acting out the parts.

> Here are two people, building houses. (*Children choose a hat and umbrella each, and put on hats, leaving their umbrellas to one side.*)
> They begin by choosing where they will build. One chooses sandy ground and the other rocky ground. (*Children stand slightly in front of the leader.*)
> They dig and dig and dig. (*Mime.*)
> They build up their houses with bricks. (*Mime.*)
> And finally they have finished their houses. (*Children stand with arms folded.*)
> But then, the rains begin. (*Spray a gentle mist over both builders.*)
> What will happen? Will the houses keep them dry? (*Children put up umbrellas as the 'rain' continues.*)
> Look! One builder is snug and dry, but the other is still getting wet – the house just isn't keeping him dry!
> The house built on sand was as useless in a storm as the umbrella with holes in it.
> Jesus said that it was when the storms came that the difference between the houses was seen – one stood firm and the other fell down.

Application

1   Draw the parallel between the story Jesus told and the idea of reading the signs and then ignoring them.
2   God has given us rules to live by and we are like the wise builder if we keep them.
3   We should read the Bible AND do what it says.

Prayer

> *God, you know that it is sometimes hard for us to do what is right. Please help us to read the Bible and to do what it says.*

Song suggestions

The baked bean song, 390, *Junior Praise*
Don't build your house on the sandy land, 39, *Junior Praise*

SPECIAL PLACES

Based on the 'Luke Street' video produced by Scripture Union, this section offers six different ways of telling the Bible narratives as an alternative to the video, and offers some ideas to be used in conjunction with it.

A good visual aid for the whole series would be a roll of lining paper with a road and each house painted on it. Unroll it a little further each time. Or simply draw the road and add a house at each assembly – you can draw and cut it out it in advance and stick it on during the assembly, without needing to have Rolf Harris' skills!

The series could lead on to class projects about houses then and now. One local community worker developed the series by taking the children and teachers, a class at a time, to her house, where they talked together, had a snack to eat and watched the video!

26 THE SICK HOUSE

Aim: To show that Jesus loves and cares for everyone.

Bible base: Luke 4:38–40. Jesus heals many people.

You will need:

- Dressing-up clothes for each character – you may be able to borrow some suitable biblical-style clothes from a local church, or use material draped and tied at the waist. You will need to dress Jesus, Peter, his wife, his mother-in-law, and other ill people who came to the house.
- You may also want some pictures of houses in Jesus' day.
- A roll of lining paper

Preparation

- Prepare the 'street on a roll' if you are using it and draw or find some pictures of appropriate houses. See *How to Cheat at Visual Aids*, published by Scripture Union, for some ideas.
- Work out how you will re-tell the story.

Presentation

Introduction

1   If this is to be the first of a series of stories from Luke Street, show pictures and talk a little about what the houses were like and how they were different from those in which we live.

2   Ask the children who would help them if they were ill. That would usually be the same for people who lived in Luke Street, but not on the day of this story, because this was the Sabbath. The Sabbath was the Jews' special day of rest, when nobody did any work.

Story

1   Ask the children to listen carefully as you read the story from the Bible because afterwards some of them will help to tell it again. Read the story from a modern translation of the Bible, such as the *Good News Bible* or *Contemporary English Version*.

2   Ask how they think the different people would have felt, and what they might have said.

3   Choose children to dress up for the different parts; then re-tell the story of the sick house in your own words (or ask the children playing parts to say words if they are able to).

Include these things:

> Jesus was interested in everyone who came to Peter's house and he had time for all those who came to be made better.

> And he made them better too, even though he wasn't a doctor!

> People must have wondered who this special man was.

Application

Still today, Jesus loves and cares for people who are ill and for their family and friends who are worried about them.

We can ask Jesus to help people who are ill and pray for those who look after them.

Ask which people today help ill people to get better.

Prayer

If appropriate, ask the children to think of anyone they know who is ill. During a short prayer that you say, asking God to help them to get better, have a moment of silence when each child can say quietly in their head the name of that person.

Say a prayer to thank God for people who help us when we are ill. If the school has a nurse, mention her/him by name.

Song suggestion

*   Jesus' hands were kind hands, 134, *Junior Praise*

27 THE RICH HOUSE

Aim: To show that Jesus forgives.

Bible base: Luke 7:36–50. Jesus at Simon the Pharisee's house.

You will need:

- A large sheet of paper or OHP acetate, and pen
- Pictures of Simon and Rebecca, to show when each is mentioned (see *How to Cheat at Visual Aids* for some ideas.)

Preparation

- Produce pictures of the two characters.
- Add the house to Luke Street if necessary.

Presentation

Introduction

Ask everyone to imagine that someone very special is coming to their house for a meal. What would they like them to eat? Write a shopping list of the special things that you might buy.

Story

Simon lived in Luke Street. He was a Pharisee, someone who taught people about God, and because of that he sometimes thought that he was also very important. He was probably quite a good man, except for thinking that he was so important. People liked him, and whenever anyone important came to dinner, he let people who lived nearby come and see the wonderful food that he gave to his guests, and to smell the delicious smells as it was cooking. Sometimes, when the meal was over, his cook might give away some of the leftovers to anyone who was still watching from the doorway.

Rebecca lived in Luke Street too, but apart from that she wasn't like Simon at all. She was not at all important, and she knew it. She wasn't really liked and she certainly wasn't a good lady. No one knew just what it was that she had done wrong, but people often turned away when they saw her coming towards them.

Rebecca was walking down Luke Street one day when she heard

Simon talking to a man she had never seen before. 'Come to my house, Jesus,' Simon was saying. 'Come to dinner tonight.' Rebecca had never been to dinner at anyone's house. In fact she had never even joined the crowds to watch Simon's guests coming and going and eating their fine food. But as she stared at the man called Jesus, he saw her watching him and he smiled at her. Rebecca didn't smile back; instead she went very red and walked away quickly.

At a quarter to six that evening the people from Luke Street started jostling for a good position in Simon's garden to see this special meal and Simon's most special guest. At five to six Simon's servants carried into Simon's dining room such delicious food that your mouth would have watered on the spot if you had seen it. In fact the noses of everyone watching twitched and flared with the wonderful smells. There was so much – and it was all perfect. At six o'clock Simon welcomed his guests at the front door, took them to the dining room, and the feast began.

Whilst Simon and Jesus were eating, Rebecca arrived at the house. Her eyes were fixed on Jesus. She didn't have to push her way to the front, because everyone seemed to melt away. She didn't wait by the door to see what happened – she just walked into the room and knelt at Jesus' feet. Jesus looked down at her and smiled: a friendly smile, and a kind smile. Rebecca started to cry. No one ever smiled at her, but this man had smiled twice in one day, and she was very, very happy – and very, very sad too. Because as he smiled, he looked right into her eyes and it was as though he could see everything she had ever done. All the times when she had tried to be good and failed – but all the times when she had chosen to be very bad too. Rebecca's tears ran down her cheeks, and dripped onto Jesus' feet, where they made little rivers through the dust from the road that was still on his feet. Rebecca was worried about that, so she wiped his feet clean with the only thing she could think of to use – her hair. Then she took a small, dark bottle that always hung round her neck, and tipped it over Jesus' feet. In it was perfume, with a sweet, strong, clean smell, that filled the whole room and drifted out into the garden.

You could have heard a pin drop in the house: no one said a word. But Simon looked very, very cross. Then Jesus spoke.

'Simon, Rebecca has done a very special thing for me, so don't turn up your nose like that. You forgot to have my feet washed, but she has washed them with her tears and wiped them with her hair. You gave me a special meal, but you'll hardly notice that the food has gone from your kitchen store. Rebecca has poured over my feet the most precious thing she has. You know that you are liked, but she needs lots of love because she has done lots of wrong things.' He looked at Rebecca and smiled again. 'All the wrong things you have done are forgiven,' he said. 'Go home and be happy.' She did, and she was.

Application

Rebecca gave up her most precious thing for Jesus. But Jesus gave to her something even more precious, that only he could give – he forgave her. The Bible says that Jesus could forgive people for the wrong things they had done because he is God's Son. The Bible says that he can still do that today. And he does forgive us, when we say that we are sorry and we mean it.

Prayer

You may want to end with a short time of quiet whilst children think if there is anything they need to be forgiven for – and then lead a simple 'sorry' prayer. Remember to include a 'thank you' to God that he does forgive us.

Song suggestion

* Father God, you love me, 17, *Spring Harvest Kids Praise 94*
* It's hard to say 'I'm sorry', 75, *Big Blue Planet*

28 THE LEADER'S HOUSE

Aim: To show that Jesus can do impossible things.

Bible base: Luke 8:40–56. Jairus and his daughter.

You will need:

* Sheets of newspaper

Preparation

• Add the house to Luke Street if necessary

Presentation

Introduction
1   Ask if any of the children thinks that they could fold a sheet of newspaper in half ten times. Let a couple try it – offer it to one of the staff to do too. Point out when they have tried, that this is impossible.
2   Sometimes we see things that we think can be done – and they cannot. Some things look impossible, but turn out to be possible after all – like riding a bike, or doing sums.
3   The story is about a father with a difficult problem.

Story
1   Tell the story of Jairus and his daughter:
– how worried and sad he felt as he saw her become ill
– how he thought that it was possible for the doctor to make her better, but instead she got worse
– how Jairus believed that it was possible Jesus could make her better, so he went to ask Jesus to come.
2   Jesus was very pleased to do that, but on the way home news came that the girl had died. Poor Jairus – now it was impossible!
3   But Jesus could do impossible things. He went to the house, told her to get up, and she did! In fact she was so well that Jesus told her parents to give her some food.

It was impossible, because the little girl was dead! But not for Jesus.

Application
1   Christians believe that when Jesus lived on earth as a man he could do impossible things because he was not just an ordinary man but God's son.
2   Christians believe too that, although it sounds impossible, Jesus is still alive today and can still do impossible things.

Prayer

Ask the children to think of things that they find hard: perhaps making friends, or doing something right.

End with a short prayer and include in it a brief silence when the children can say in their head what it is that they find hard.

> *Jesus, you can do impossible things and you can help us when we find something hard to do. Please help us today with these things... Amen.*

Song suggestion

• My God is so big, so strong and so mighty, 169, *Junior Praise*

29 THE GUEST HOUSE

Aim: To help the children to appreciate that friendship (with each other and with Jesus) requires an investment of time.

Bible base: Luke 10:38–42. Jesus visits Martha and Mary.

You will need:

A long-handled sweeping brush

Preparation

• Practise the story.
• Add the house to Luke Street if necessary.

Presentation

Introduction

1 Discover from the children what happens at home when someone is coming to visit. Talk about preparations that are made.

2 Explain that when a very dusty room is swept (BRUSH, BRUSH) the cloud of dust can cause the cleaner to cough (COUGH, COUGH). This in turn could lead to a sneeze (ATISHOO) – 'POOR YOU!'

3 Remind them of the way that houses and roads in Luke Street were built and of how dusty the house would get from the road outside.

4   In this story a lady called Martha will get out her broom to sweep the floor. Every time Martha says 'Oh no, I'm going to have to get the broom out,' everyone should join in and say
BRUSH, BRUSH, COUGH, COUGH, ATISHOO, POOR YOU!
Have everyone practise before starting the story.

Story

Martha and Mary were two sisters who lived in the little town of Bethany when Jesus was alive. In fact they were his friends.

They were busy round the house because they were expecting Jesus and some of his friends to come today.

'Perhaps he'll stay the night,' said Martha.

'Let's get out the spare bed rolls,' suggested Mary. They pulled the rolls out from the chest and shook them up.

Mary said, 'We need some food. I'll go and start the cooking.' As she walked away Martha looked down at the floor. Where the bed rolls had been shaken there was now dust. When they had pulled them out of the chest, some straw had fallen to the floor.

Martha said, 'Oh no, I'm going to have to get the broom out!'

She went BRUSH, BRUSH, COUGH, COUGH, ATISHOO, POOR YOU!

By this time Mary had almost finished cooking some bread. She had used flour. When Martha reached the oven the loaves were just going in. Mary said, 'I'm going to see if Jesus is coming. I'll look outside.'

As she walked away Martha looked at the floor. There was lots of spilt flour.

Martha said, 'Oh no, I'm going to have to get the broom out!'

She went BRUSH, BRUSH, COUGH, COUGH, ATISHOO, POOR YOU!

Mary shouted, 'He's coming!' and both sisters ran down the dusty road to meet Jesus. There were so many questions – 'How are you?' – 'You can stay the night, can't you?' – 'Would you like some of the food we have made for you.'

Jesus walked into the house from the dusty road. Mary walked into the house from the dusty road. They sat down together and started to talk.

Martha walked into the house from the dusty road and saw loads of dusty footprints.

Martha said, 'Oh no, I'm going to have to get the broom out!'
She went BRUSH, BRUSH, COUGH, COUGH, ATISHOO, POOR
YOU!

Mary was still talking to Jesus. Then Martha remembered the
cooking. 'The loaves! They're still in the oven!' She ran in and in the
hurry forgot to use the cloth as she lifted the tray out from the heat.
She burnt her fingers – 'Ouch!' and shook them. The loaves flew up
in the air, turned two somersaults and crashed onto the floor. They
turned to crumbs.
Martha said, 'Oh no, I'm going to have to get the broom out!'
She went BRUSH, BRUSH, COUGH, COUGH, ATISHOO, POOR
YOU!

Mary was still talking to Jesus. Martha realised that there was now
nothing to give Jesus to eat, so she quickly got more flour to bake
new loaves. She rushed and rushed and rushed. The kitchen got
messier and messier and messier. She put the new loaves in to bake.
She looked at the state of the floor.
Martha said, 'Oh no, I'm going to have to get the broom out!'
Then she went, 'NO!'

No! Why should I? she thought. I've done all the sweeping and the
cleaning since Jesus arrived. I've done the cooking now as well. It's
not fair. My sister's just sitting in there talking to Jesus. I'm going in
there and I'm going to say 'Master, will you tell my sister, it's not fair.
I've done all the work and she's just sitting talking to you.'

So she did. Jesus smiled at Martha with a very understanding smile.
He said 'Martha, I know you're doing all these things because you
want the best for me – but I've not come to see if your food is the
best in the world. I've not come to see if your house is the tidiest in
the village. I've come to see you and to hear your news – and for
you to hear mine. If we don't talk, that can't happen. Just at the
moment Mary has chosen the right thing. Now why don't you put
the broom away and come and join us.'

So she did. Well, after she'd taken the bread out of the oven!

Application

1   Being friends takes time. We need to spend time with our friends

and talk and listen to them. We need to do that with Jesus too if he is to be our friend.

2   We can do that by looking at the Bible and hearing stories about him, and by talking to him. Christians call this prayer.

3   People sometimes think that they should only talk to Jesus about big and important things, but Jesus is interested in everything that happens to us, so we can talk to him about anything.

Prayer

Ask the children to imagine that Jesus was sitting next to them. What would they say to him?

Ask them to sit quietly for a moment and, in their heads, to say those things to Jesus.

Afterwards, say 'Amen' to show that the time is over.

Song suggestion

•   Jesus is a friend of mine, 136, *Junior Praise*

30 THE SECRET HOUSE

Aim: To teach about Jesus' death

Bible base: Luke 22:7–23:56. The Last Supper and the Crucifixion.

You will need:

•   A cake or some sort of party food (the packaging alone would do)
•   A bread roll and a glass of blackcurrant juice

Preparation

Add the house to Luke Street.

Presentation

Introduction

1   Talk about a time when a friend was – or you were – moving away and you had to say goodbye. Show the party food/cake and explain how you had a special leaving party because you were saying goodbye to special friends.

2   Tell the story of how Jesus and the disciples ate a special meal together. Afterwards, Jesus gave them some bread to eat and some wine to drink and told them to remember him. (Show the bread roll and blackcurrant juice as you talk – perhaps break up the bread and give it to some of the staff.)

Story

Jesus knew that this was their last meal together. Even though Jesus was the Son of God who never did anything wrong, he knew that he was going to die the next day.

Not only had he never done anything wrong, Jesus had done lots of very good things – but not everyone liked Jesus. There were some important people who wanted to be rid of him.

Even though Jesus had made ill people better and forgiven people who had done wrong, (remind the children of other stories from this series) and even though this was Jesus the Son of God who never did anything wrong, some men decided to make sure that he was arrested and killed.

After their special supper, Jesus and his friends went out for a walk. While they were out, soldiers came and arrested Jesus. They took him to the important people, who told lies about him and made up untrue stories about him. The next day Jesus, the Son of God who never did anything wrong, was taken to a hillside outside the city, and was killed. Jesus died, nailed to a wooden cross.

His friends and lots of other people too were so very, very sad. This was Jesus who had done so much for them and who had loved them. And now he was dead.

Even the soldier who was in charge of it all decided that Jesus really was the Son of God.

So the meal at the Secret House really had been a goodbye party after all.

But the story goes on further, as I think you know.

Tell the rest of it in another assembly! Don't leave the children thinking that Jesus' death was the end of it all.

Prayer

Jesus, please help me to understand more about you.

Song suggestion

• Jesus is a friend of mine, 136, *Junior Praise*

31 THE COUNTRY HOUSE

Aim: To help the children to grasp the wonderful fact that although Jesus died, he came alive again!

Bible base: Luke 24:13–49. Jesus appears to his friends.

You will need:

• Two large signs, one saying 'Yes' and the other 'No'

Preparation

• Make the two signs and practise telling the story with plenty of opportunities to use them – or simply use the script below.
• Add the house to Luke Street.

Presentation

Introduction

1   If this is the last in the series of stories from Luke Street, remind the children of the others, either by showing the road of houses or by mentioning the names and asking if they can remember what happened at each.

Whether you do this or not, set the scene for the story with a reminder of Jesus' death and how sad his friends were about it. If you can, put across the sense of aching distress and loss that the disciples must have felt that someone so good, who gave himself to others so completely, had been killed.

2   Explain that you need help to tell the story: you would like the children to join in with the words as you show the cards. Practise by asking 'Do you think you can do that?' and holding up the 'yes' card for the answer, and 'Or is that too hard?' and the 'no' card. Explain that when you hold up the card during the story the children are to say 'yes' or 'no'.

Story

It was Sunday evening, and two friends of Jesus were in Jerusalem. They were very confused. On the Friday morning they had seen Jesus nailed to a cross. On the Friday afternoon he had died and been buried. On Saturday, the special day of rest, they and his other friends had sat together and talked about all the good things that Jesus had done, and they had cried together because their friend was dead. But then this morning some of the women had been to Jesus' tomb and seen that his body wasn't there – and two angels had told them that now he was alive again!

'Do you want to stay longer?' asked one of the friends.
'**NO**,' said Cleopas, 'I'm ready to go home. Are you?'
'**YES**,' came the answer, and they set off to walk seven miles back to their home in the village of Emmaus.
'It's been an amazing day,' said Cleopas. 'Do you understand it all?'
'**NO**,' said his friend, 'I don't.' They began to talk about Jesus and all that had happened.

They were still talking when someone else joined them on the road. It was getting dark, so they couldn't see him clearly, but he was friendly and asked if he could walk with them.
'**YES**,' they both answered, 'you're welcome.'
'What were you talking about?' the man asked. They stopped for a moment and looked very sad.
'Haven't you heard what's happened in Jerusalem these last few days?' asked Cleopas.
'**NO**,' said the man, 'tell me all about it.' So they did – all about Jesus and the things he had done, about how special he had been, and how he had died but now, perhaps, was alive again.

The man said 'Can I tell you something very important?'

'Oh, **YES** please!' said the other two. The man began to explain about how for hundreds and hundreds of years God had told people about his Son and all that he would do.

He was still talking when they arrived at Emmaus and he began to say goodbye.

'**NO**, don't go!' said Cleopas, 'You could stay with us for some food and stay the night too. It's getting late. Will you stay?'

'**YES**,' said the man. 'I'd love to.'

They sat down to eat together.

'Please would you say thank you to God for the food?' asked Cleopas.

'**YES**, of course,' said the man. He picked up the bread in his hands, said thank you to God for it, broke it into pieces and began to share it out.

'That's just how Jesus used to do it,' thought Cleopas. 'This man reminds me so much of Jesus... he's just like him... in fact, **YES!**' he shouted, 'it is Jesus!' And at that moment Jesus left them and they were alone again.

'It was Jesus! It was Jesus!' they shouted. '**YES! YES! YES!** Jesus really is alive, and he was here with us!' They were so excited that they left the table and left their meal and ran all the way back to Jerusalem, all seven miles. They went straight to the house where their friends had met.

'Guess what!' said the others, 'Jesus is alive – Peter's met him!'

'**YES**,' shouted the two friends. '**YES**, we know – he came to supper with us! Isn't it wonderful?'

'**YES!**' shouted all the friends together.

Application

You might think it's impossible that Jesus could be alive again when he really was dead. (Remind the children of the 'Impossible Things' story of Jesus at Jairus' house if you have told that one.) You might think '**NO**, he couldn't possibly be alive again.'

But the Bible says '**YES**', Jesus did come alive again. Christians believe that '**YES**', the Bible is true; that '**YES**', even though we can't see Jesus with our eyes or touch him with our hands, he is still alive today and '**YES**', he is God's Son who wants to be our friend.

Prayer

Thank you, God, that Jesus came alive again, and so because of that he can even be in our streets. Please help us to understand more about him.

Song suggestions

- Jesus is greater than the greatest heroes, 10, *Spring Harvest Kids' Praise 1992*
- Hosanna, Hosanna, 38, *Big Blue Planet*

SECTION 6

SPECIAL TIMES

32 PARTY TIME!

Aim: To show that Jesus enjoyed parties too!

Bible base: John 2:1–11. The wedding party at Cana.

You will need:

- Things to set up as if for a party – plates, cups, serviettes, party hats, candles etc – anything you have to make it look different from an ordinary meal
- You might want to find some suitable clothes or hats for the children who take part to wear
- A modern translation of the Bible (*Good News Bible* or *Contemporary English Version*)

Presentation

Introduction

1   Tell the children that you are getting ready for something special. Can they guess what? What kind of a party might it be? Has anyone been to a wedding? Has anyone been a bridesmaid or page boy? What happens at the party after the wedding?

2   Read the story from a modern translation of the Bible.

3   Choose helpers to act out the wedding: Jesus, Mary, bride, groom, three servants, head servant. Re-tell the story, helping the characters to act it out – the action is fairly obvious.

Story

Jesus went to a wedding with his mother and his friends. It was a lovely party – everyone enjoyed themselves, and everyone was very happy. But then, oh dear! Before the party was over, the wine ran out and there was no more to drink.

Jesus' mother went to talk to him. 'There is no more wine,' she said. Then to the servants she said, 'Do whatever Jesus tells you.'

'Fill the water jars,' said Jesus. So they did. 'Now, take some to the man in charge of the party.'

The man tasted the drink and looked so pleased. 'Why, this is the very best wine!' he said.

Jesus gave the people a very special present and helped them to have a very special party that day!

Application
People sometimes think Jesus must have been a very serious man, but like many of us, he obviously went to and enjoyed parties.

Prayer
End with a prayer thanking God for parties and other special times.

Song suggestion
- Jesus' love is very wonderful, 139, *Junior Praise*

33 HARVEST – SHARING

Aim: To show the children that God has given us good things which are to be shared.

Bible base: 1 Kings 17:7–24. Elijah and the widow.

You will need:
- Sultanas
- Suitable props for the characters, eg a scarf for the woman, a stick for Elijah

Presentation

Introduction
1   Ask for two volunteers who like sultanas and share them out unfairly between them and you – make sure you get most and that they have just one or two each. Ask them to share theirs with others. Are they keen to do so? Why? Comment on the unfairness of the distribution and even it out.

2   It is easier to share something if you have lots, and much harder if you have just a small amount. Ask the children which things are easy to share and which are hard. Talk about how sharing means that everyone gets something.

Story
Tell the story of Elijah and the widow, using the different props.

> Elijah was a man who knew God, talked to God and did what God told him to do. One day God told Elijah to go to a town called Zarephath, and to stay with a lady and her son there.
>
> When Elijah got to Zarephath he saw the woman coming towards him. She was collecting sticks to burn on her fire.
>
> 'Please give me a drink of water,' said Elijah, 'and some bread to eat.'
>
> 'I have no bread,' said the lady. 'There is just enough flour in my bowl and oil in my jar to make one last meal for me and my son, and then we will die because we have no more food.'
>
> There had been no rain there for a very long time and now there was very little food for everyone.
>
> 'Don't worry,' said Elijah. 'Just make your meal, but first make a small loaf for me. God says that until it rains again, there will always be enough flour in the bowl and oil in the jar.'
>
> The lady did as Elijah said. She shared her meal by making some bread for him and then some for herself and her son. Every time she made the bread, there was always enough flour and always enough oil. From that day until it rained again, they had just enough food to eat.

Application
Remind the children of how hard it is to share something when you have very little of it. The lady had almost nothing left, but she shared it with Elijah, and God was pleased with her.

You might want to leave a small bag of sultanas for each class, to make the point more clearly!

Prayer

End with a prayer asking God to help us to share, even when it is hard to do so.

Song suggestion

• Someone's brought a loaf of bread, 220, *Junior Praise*

34 HARVEST THANKSGIVING

Aim: To teach that harvest is a time to thank God for all that he gives to us.

You will need:

- A loaf of bread, and all the ingredients for a loaf: flour, oil yeast, water
- If you can get hold of a copy, you could tell the story from *Thank you for a loaf of bread* which was published by Lion Publishing but is now out of print
- An OHP acetate or large sheet of paper, and pen

Preparation

None – unless you want to bake your own loaf!

Presentation

1   Who had toast for breakfast? Or bread? Did they enjoy it? And who will have sandwiches for lunch? What is their favourite filling?

2   We often eat food without stopping to say thank you for it. We are going to say thank you for all the people who gave us our bread. But where do we begin? Choose one of the children who had bread for breakfast and ask them to help you to work it all out. Write out the different people involved on a long list on the OHP or large paper.

> Who made their breakfast? (Mum/Dad) So it's 'Thank you...'
> But they got the bread from somewhere – where?
> (Shop/supermarket) So it's 'Thank you for the shopkeeper'.
> But they got the bread from the baker, so it's 'Thank you for the baker'.
> But the baker made the bread from different things. (Show the flour, oil, yeast and water.)
> Flour comes from wheat that has been ground down, so it's 'Thank you for the miller'.
> But before the miller can grind the flour, the wheat has to have grown strong and ripe, so it's 'Thank you for the farmer who grew the wheat'.

Wheat needs sun and rain, and it's God who makes the sun to shine and the rain to fall. So in the end it's 'Thank you, God'.

Application
Harvest is a special time to say thank you to God for all the good things we have, which he has given to us.

Prayer

Thank you, God, for sun and rain, for grass and wheat, for farmers and millers, for bakers, shopkeepers and for the people who look after us and make our meals for us. And thank you for a loaf of bread.

Song suggestion

- Thank you Lord for this fine day, 232, *Junior Praise* (including verses with 'food' words chosen by the children)

35 LIGHT

This assembly has been included to be used where a positive alternative to Hallowe'en is wanted. It focusses on Jesus the light who has overcome the darkness.

Aim: To explain that Jesus is like a light, and that his light never goes out.

Bible base: John 1:5 and 8:12

You will need:

- Lots of different sources of light – torch, lamp, match and candle, bicycle light, etc
- A scarf as a blindfold

Presentation

1   Set up a simple – and safe! – assault course, eg under a chair and over a low table.

Ask for a volunteer to go through it. When they have done this successfully, ask them to do it again, but blindfold. If they do, guide them carefully and ask at the end how it felt, and which was easier. If they won't try it blindfold, simply make the point that it can be frightening to have to do things when we can't see.

2   Talk about how scared people can get in the dark – grown-ups too! – and how even a bit of light helps. Somehow all the things that seem scary at night go away when there is a light on or when it is morning.

People are not frightened of the light. Show the different sorts of lights and talk about where and how they might be used.

Application
1   Jesus said, 'I am the light of the world'.
2   Christians believe that Jesus can help us when we are frightened. The Bible says, 'The light shines in the darkness, and the darkness has never put it out'. Jesus is that light which can never be put out.

Prayer

Ask the children to join in the prayer by saying 'Help me, please, Jesus' after you have said 'Jesus, you're the Light, so...'

> *Sometimes it's dark and I feel alone. But Jesus, you're the Light, so*
> *Help me, please, Jesus.*
> *Sometimes it's dark and I feel scared. But Jesus, you're the Light, so*
> *Help me, please, Jesus.*
> *Sometimes it's dark and I am frightened by strange noises in the night or*
> *by how quiet the house is. But Jesus, you're the Light, so*
> *Help me, please, Jesus.*

Song suggestion

•   I am the light, the light of the world, 34, *Everybody Praise*

36 GET READY! (ADVENT)

Aim: To help the children to think about getting ready for Christmas, and what Christmas is about.

Bible base: Isaiah 9:6, Matthew 1 and Luke 1. The birth of Jesus.

You will need:

A bag of objects which give clues to special events eg sunglasses and suntan cream for a holiday; some baby powder and a bib for a new baby; some make-up and a hat for a wedding; some decorations and an Advent calendar

Presentation

Introduction

1   Play a guessing game with the objects in the bag, asking what the children think you might be getting ready for with each pair of things.

2   Ask what they have seen happening as people get ready for Christmas – shopping, baking, putting up decorations etc.

Story

Christmas is the time when people celebrate Jesus being born as a baby. Hundreds of years before Jesus was born at the first Christmas, God helped people to be ready for his coming. He sent lots of different people as messengers to tell everyone to be ready, because one day God's special person would come.

These are some of the words that one of them, Isaiah, said. 'A child is born to us! A son is given to us! And he will be our ruler. He will be called "Wonderful Counsellor", "Mighty God", "Eternal Father", "Prince of Peace".' (Isaiah 9:6, *Good News Bible*)

Finally God sent an angel to tell Mary to get ready, because this wonderful baby would be born to her.

Show again the baby things that you have, and explain how Mary would not have got these sort of things together to be ready, but she would have made some preparations.

God also sent a message to Joseph, to tell him to get ready for the coming of Jesus, this very special baby.

Application

1   Ask why they think God went to so much trouble, telling people to get ready.
2   Explain that Jesus was born so we could know God better and understand how much he loves us.
3   Christians call this time of year Advent, a time to be ready for Jesus' coming. Suggest that as the children get ready for Christmas they remember the coming of Jesus too. If they have an Advent calendar at home they could remember Jesus as they open the door each day.

Prayer

Ask the children for ideas of what excites them about getting ready for Christmas, and use these as a short prayer to say 'thank you' to God for each of these, and for Jesus.

Song suggestion

*   'Twas early Christmas morning, 35, *Big Blue Planet*
*   Come and join the celebration, 323, *Junior Praise*

37 PASS THE CHRISTMAS PARCELS

Aim: To explain clearly the facts surrounding the birth of Jesus.

Bible base: Matthew 1 & 2, Luke 1 & 2. The birth of Jesus.

You will need:

- the following items to wrap and number as shown:
    1. A 'decree' – wording as suggested by Luke 2:1–3
    2. A map showing Nazareth and Bethlehem (a simple drawing will do)
    3. A 'No Room' sign
    4. Some straw
    5. A toy donkey
    6. A doll wrapped up in cloths as Jesus would have been
    7. An angel (a Christmas decoration or paper one)
    8. A toy sheep
    9. A star
    10. A box to represent one of the gifts given to Jesus
    11. A question mark
- Christmas paper
- a tape of suitable music and cassette player
- a rubbish bag for all the paper!

Preparation

Wrap each item from the list in Christmas paper and number them in the correct order for the story.

Some can be omitted to cut down on time, but the larger number means that everyone should at least handle a parcel.

Presentation

Introduction

1   Ask what games the children like playing at Christmas parties. Make sure 'Pass the Parcel' is mentioned.

2   Explain that today's game will be played slightly differently: all the parcels will be passed around together and, when the music stops, you will call out the numbers of the parcels that you want to be opened.

3   Spread out the parcels among the children and give clear instructions about which way they are to be passed. When the music stops, call out two numbers at a time (otherwise it takes too long!) and have the children bring the parcels to the front to be opened.

4   As each parcel is opened, tell the relevant part of the story.

Story

Begin with music. Open parcels 1 and 2.

> Long ago, when Augustus was Emperor, he decided to take a count of everyone who lived in the country of Judea. *(Show the decree)*
>
> Two people, Mary and Joseph had to travel from Nazareth, where they lived, to Bethlehem, where Joseph's family came from many years before. *(Show the map)*

Music. Open parcels 3 and 4.

> When they got to Bethlehem, the town was so busy with travellers like themselves that all the places to stay were full *(Show the sign)*, and Mary and Joseph had to stay in a stable, and sleep in the straw. *(Show the straw)*

Music. Open parcels 5 and 6.

> During the night, Mary's baby son was born. He was called Jesus. There was nowhere for him to sleep except the manger, the feeding trough that the cows and donkeys used. *(Show the donkey)* Mary wrapped up Jesus in strips of cloth, and laid him in the straw. *(Show the baby)*

Music and parcels 7 and 8.

> Jesus, the baby born in the stable, was not just any baby: he was the Son of God. Later that night angels *(Show the angel)* went to tell the good news of Jesus' birth to some shepherds. *(Show the sheep)*

Music and parcels 9 and 10.

> A special star came in the sky too *(Show the star)*, and some wise men who studied the sky saw the star, and followed it many, many miles until it took them to the place where Jesus was. When they saw the baby Jesus they gave him special presents of gold, incense and myrrh. *(Show the gift)* These gifts were not what you might take to a newborn baby; but they were just right for someone so special, like Jesus.

Music and parcel 11.

Application

1   When the question mark is opened, ask the children why they think God sent Jesus to live on earth.

2   Explain that Jesus was God's special present to us, because he loves us so much.

Prayer

Ask the children to join in by saying 'Thank you, Father God' after every line.

> *It's Christmas time, and we're excited:*
> > *Thank you, Father God.*
> *There are lots of things that make us delighted:*
> > *Thank you, Father God.*
> *For our families and our friends:*
> > *Thank you, Father God.*
> *For your love, that never ends:*
> > *Thank you, Father God.*
> *For excitement and fun:*
> > *Thank you, Father God.*
> *And for Jesus, your Son:*
> > *Thank you, Father God.*

Song suggestion

- Christmas, it's Christmas, 9, *Everybody Praise*
- Christ was born in Bethlehem, 36, *Big Blue Planet*
- Come and join the celebration, 323, *Junior Praise*

38 NEW YEAR, NEW BEGINNINGS

Aim: To show that, with God, a new start is always possible.

Bible base: Luke 15:11–24. The Lost Son.

You will need:

- a large sheet of paper
- poster paints
- a paint brush
- something to protect the floor etc
- an easel would be helpful

Preparation

None essential (but you could draw a faint outline for the painting, to make it easier!).

Presentation

Introduction

1   You do not need to be a good artist for this! Paint a picture; it looks good to begin with, but as you get carried away using colours you forget to wash the brush and the colours begin to run together. Don't spend too long on it. Hold it up to show people; as you do so, the paint will run and the picture will be spoiled some more.

2   Start again, asking someone to help and advise you. Perhaps use a staff member who is artistic.

3   Some things can never be started again. But some can. You were able to start the picture again, and the person you asked to help stopped you from making the same mistakes again.

4   This is the start of a new year. It's fresh and new, like a clean sheet of paper. Just as you asked for help to get the painting right, we can ask God, who makes each day new, to help us to get things right. And he will. But even when we get things wrong, God can help us to start again.

The assembly could end after this, or go on to tell the story of the lost son if you want to take the subject further.

If you are very artistic, the second picture could be of a dad and his son!

Story
Tell the story of the dad and the son. You might want to have some words for the children to join in every time you mention the two characters – eg 'Dad...' said in pleading voice, for the son; 'Yes, son' for the dad.

There was once a dad who had two sons. One was older, so, of course the other one was younger. One day the younger son went to his dad and said 'DAD...' 'YES, SON,' said the father. 'DAD... could I have my share of your money now please?'

His dad thought about it for a while, and then, even though he didn't want to see his son leave home, he said, 'YES, SON,' because he loved him.

The son set off for a country far away and quickly spent the money on parties, food, and all sorts of other things that he'd always wanted for himself. But it didn't last for ever, and finally he ran out of money.

He got himself a job; not a very good job, just feeding pigs. But then there was no food in the country and he began to get very, very hungry.

At last he realised what a mess he'd made of everything. And then he started to get things right.

He decided to go home and say 'sorry' to his dad, and ask his dad to let him work as a servant. So he set off for home.

Even before he got home, while he was still practising what he would say to his dad, his father saw him coming and ran to meet him. 'DAD...' began the boy, wanting to go on to say all the things about being a servant. But his dad was so pleased to see him that he interrupted. 'YES, SON,' he said, 'It's great to see you and I'm so glad that you're back. Let's have a party everybody!'

So they did. Even though the boy had wasted all the money, his dad welcomed him back because he loved the boy so much.

What was it that the boy needed to say to his father? Sorry.

Why did the dad welcome his son home and let him start again? Because he loved him.

Application

Jesus told that story to help people to understand that God is like the father in the story. When we have done things wrong and made a mess of things, we can go to him and say 'sorry' – and because he loves us he will forgive us and give us a new beginning.

Prayer

It may be appropriate to end with a 'sorry' prayer, but include with it a 'thank you' that God does forgive and help us to start again, and perhaps a 'please' that he will help us to get things right.

Song suggestion

• Jesus is the living way, 9, *Spring Harvest Kids Praise 94*

39 DOGGER (EASTER)

Note: As well as telling the facts of what happened when Jesus died on the cross the Bible also explains why Jesus died – what God achieved through his death. The theological word is 'redemption' – God 'buying back' people who were lost to him. It's a word that was used to describe the process by which people were freed from slavery. When applied to God and humankind it makes clear how precious we are to God – that he would give up his only son to help us.

Jesus often told stories to explain truths about God. The story 'Dogger', which is probably well known to infants, is a lovely illustration of this: a child giving up a teddy to get back her brother's lost precious toy dog. It falls short of what God did for us: Bella didn't really like the teddy, whereas it cost God dearly to give up Jesus. This assembly attempts to explain what Jesus' death means, and how precious we are to God.

Bible base: Ephesians 2:13

You will need:

- *Dogger* by Shirley Hughes, published by Picture Lions/Collins
- You may also want to use a toy dog to illustrate the story

Preparation

- Edit the story to a manageable length.

Presentation

Most children will be familiar with the story, but tell your edited version, showing the pictures as appropriate. The key points to include are:

- Dogger was very precious to Dave.
- Dave was devastated when Dogger was lost and searched long and hard for him.
- Dave wanted to buy back Dogger as soon as he saw him on the stall.
- By giving up something special Bella was able to reunite Dave with Dogger.

Because Dogger was so precious to Dave, Bella was prepared to give up the teddy bear she had won so that Dave and Dogger could be together.

The Bible says that people were made to have a friendship with God. But the wrong things we do spoil it, and make it as if we are lost.

Application

People who didn't like Jesus killed him and he died on a cross. But God did something very special. Because we are so precious to God, he used what they did to get us back, like Bella got back Dogger for Dave. So we can be with God for ever.

Actually, Bella didn't like the teddy all that much, so it wasn't too hard for her.

The Bible says that God loved Jesus very much, and it must have been very hard for him to let him die. But we are so special that he was willing to do it to get back our friendship.

That's what Easter is all about: remembering Jesus dying on the cross and how, because of that, we can be with God for ever.

Prayer

Thank you, God, that we are precious to you. And thank you for Jesus, who shows us just how much you love us.

Song suggestions

- I'm special, 106, *Junior Praise*
- Jesus' love is very wonderful, 139, *Junior Praise*
- For God so loved the world, 4, *Spring Harvest Kids Praise 1994*

40 HAPPY BIRTHDAY, DEAR CHURCH (PENTECOST)

Aim: To explain about the Holy Spirit, Jesus' present to those who follow him.

Bible base: Acts 1:4–8; 2:1–14. The coming of the Holy Spirit.

You will need:

- A cake with birthday candles on it
- Signs saying 'Holy Spirit' and 'Power'

Preparation

- Wrap the signs in gift wrap, preferably some that is clearly marked 'birthday'.

Presentation

Introduction

1 Enquire if it is anyone's birthday today... or this week.

2 Talk about birthdays and what we receive ie cards, presents, cake etc.

3   Show the birthday cake and light the candles. Begin to sing 'Happy Birthday' but stop as you begin the line 'Happy Birthday dear...'
(Sing it through first for any who have had a birthday that week, and then ask the children to sing it once again, stopping as above.)
4   Christians call the special time of year known as 'Pentecost' the birthday of the church. Explain how 'the church' is not just the building where people meet on a Sunday (mention a local church by name) but is a name given to everyone in the world who follows Jesus.

Story
Tell the story from Acts 1 and 2, in particular how:
1   Jesus was leaving his special friends and going back to be with God.
2   He promised to send the Holy Spirit, his helper, to be with them.
3   All of Jesus' followers were in a room together in Jerusalem. There was a sound like a strong wind blowing, that seemed to fill the house, and they saw what looked like little flames dancing around on each person.
4   The Holy Spirit had come, just as Jesus promised. Unwrap the 'Holy Spirit' sign.
Jesus said that when the Holy Spirit came, he would give them a special present. Unwrap the 'Power' sign and go on to tell what happened next.
5   Jesus' friends began to talk in foreign languages, even though they had never learned to speak them. (You may want to say a few suitable phrases in some foreign languages eg 'Lobe den Herrn' – 'Praise to the Lord' in German or 'Clod i Dduw' – Welsh for 'Praise to God' – *pronounced 'clowd', to rhyme with 'crow', 'ee', 'thew', to rhyme with dew, with a hard 'th' as in 'the'*.)
6   People from lots of foreign countries, who were in Jerusalem and were outside the house, could hear them talking, and understood them!
7   Peter was very brave and bold: he stood up in front of thousands of people and told them all about Jesus.

Application
1   Jesus had already told his disciples about the Holy Spirit, how he was like the wind – you can't see it, but you can see what it does. Ask the children if they can see your breath as you blow into the air.

They can't. Ask them to watch what happens as you blow on the candles.

2   We can't see the Holy Spirit, but he is Jesus' special present to those who follow him, to be with them and to make them brave to do what is right, just as he made Peter brave.

3   Re-light the candles and sing 'Happy Birthday, dear Church'.

Prayer

Ask the children to join in with the words 'Thank you, God' at the end of each line.

> *For birthdays and parties*
> > *Thank you, God.*
> *For fun and enjoyment*
> > *Thank you, God.*
> *For presents and happiness*
> > *Thank you, God.*
> *For your Holy Spirit*
> > *Thank you, God.*

Song suggestion

•   Jesus, send me the Helper, 409, *Junior Praise*

41 THE HOLIDAY STARTS HERE! (END OF SCHOOL YEAR)

Aim: To help the children to grasp that God, who is greater than we can ever imagine, knows all about us and watches over us wherever we go.

Bible base: Psalm 139:9–10

You will need:

- An outline of Britain – on an acetate, or drawn large if an OHP is not available
- A globe
- Marker pens
- A road map of Britain (with index!) in case you need to look up any destinations
- A suitcase containing some of the things you would take on holiday
- A large sign, which will fit in the case, saying 'God'

Preparation

Know your geography!

Presentation

Introduction

1 Who is excited about finishing school for the summer? (Be sure to let the staff say so too!)
Who is going away on holiday? What will they take with them? Show the things you have packed.
2 Ask for the names of some of the places people are going to and mark them on the map with that person's name. Be sure also to mark on those who are having their holiday at home. Point out foreign destinations on the globe. How will they get to where they are going?

Story

1 Talk about some of the people in the Bible who went on long journeys – Abraham going to a new country; Joseph going as a slave into Egypt; Moses leading the people to God's special land; Joseph and Mary taking Jesus to safety in Egypt when he was a baby; Paul going on long journeys to tell people about Jesus. Each one knew that wherever they went, God was with them.

2 Read the verses from Psalm 139.
'If I flew away beyond the east or lived in the farthest place in the west, you would be there to lead me, you would be there to help me.' (Psalm 139:9–10, *Good News Bible*)

Application

Show the 'God' sign from your suitcase. We can't see God with our eyes or hear him with our ears or feel him with our hands – but he will be with us always if we ask him to be, just as he was with these people.

It doesn't matter where we go in the world: God is so great that he can be everywhere with anyone.

When we come back to school next year from summer holidays, when we go to new classes – or even new schools – God will still watch over and care for each one.

Prayer

Say a short prayer thanking God for holidays at home and away, and, if appropriate, asking him to be close to children who are going to a new school.

Song suggestions

- If you climb to the top of a mountain, 388, *Junior Praise*
- He's got the whole world in his hands, 78, *Junior Praise*
- Father God you love me, 3, *Spring Harvest Kids Praise 1994*

Other Resources from Scripture Union

Storytelling: A practical guide
Lance Pierson

Guidance on how to bring stories to life, use
them creatively and make them exciting and
thought-provoking. Includes a helpful chapter on
the importance of reading the Bible aloud in
church, and how this can be done in an effective
and stimulating way.
ISBN 1 85999 094 0
£5.99

How to Cheat at Visual Aids!
Pauline Adams & Judith Merrell

People remember 30% of what they hear, but
60% of what they see and hear – that makes
this guide to producing visual aids
indispensable. Over 500 pictures of New
Testament characters and stories.
PHOTOCOPIABLE
ISBN 0 86201 990 7
£6.99

How to Cheat at Visual Aids! Old Testament
Pauline Adams & Judith Merrell

A follow-on from the well-received How to
Cheat at Visual Aids, this volume deals
specifically with Old Testament people, events
and festivals. May be used with the original
How to Cheat... or alone.
PHOTOCOPIABLE
ISBN 1 85999 161 0
£7.99